W9-BLV-557

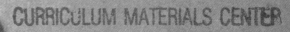

Lincoln
through the Lens

HOW PHOTOGRAPHY REVEALED AND SHAPED AN EXTRAORDINARY LIFE

Martin W. Sandler

WALKER & COMPANY

New York

Introduction

He was born in a humble log cabin but rose to the highest office in the land. He had almost no formal education but earned a place in history as one of the most eloquent leaders the world has ever known. He held a nation together during its most bitter and tragic conflict but became the last, great casualty of that war.

His name was Abraham Lincoln, and his early life gave little indication of the greatness that was to come. He opened a general store, but it failed. He ran for local office, but he lost. He became a rail-splitter, a river boatman, and a village postmaster, but none of these jobs satisfied him.

Yet, despite his humble beginnings, his lack of schooling, and his early failures, he was a man determined to make something of himself. "I'm a slow walker," he said, "but I never walk back." Asked about his family background he replied, "I don't know who my grandfather was; I am much more concerned to know who his grandson will be."

He was tall and ungainly, with features that were far from handsome. But he had an extraordinary sense of humor. The stories and jokes he told would become known not only for the laughter they brought but also for the wisdom often contained within them. Asked why he was often so quiet, he replied, "Better to remain silent and be thought a fool than to speak out and remove all doubt."

He loved to laugh, and he loved to make others laugh as well. But all who knew him were aware that there was also a deep sadness about him, a melancholy that would remain with him all his life. "I laugh because I must not weep," he told a friend. "What is tired in me lies within, and can't be got at," he confided to another.

His sadness while president was understandable. He had been called on to lead the nation that he loved so much at a time when its very future was seriously in doubt. But under circumstances that would have weakened the resolve of lesser men, he remained true to his awesome responsibilities.

He was on the national stage for only six years. But in that time this complex man from the heart of the frontier kept the American nation from destroying itself. His greatest strength came from his unwavering faith in the common man. "I am a firm believer in the people," he would proclaim. "If given the truth, they can be depended upon to meet any national crisis. The great point is to bring them the real facts."

Two hundred years after his birth, myths about Abraham Lincoln still abound. And no wonder. "Lincoln," the poet Carl Sandburg wrote, "was too big and too complicated to be painted in a few strokes. . . . You cannot picture him in simple lines." Perhaps the late nineteenth-century lawyer and orator Robert Ingersoll said it best. "Lincoln," he proclaimed, "was not a type. He stands alone—no ancestors, no fellows, no successors."

2

A Historic Discovery

"Four score and seven years ago our fathers brought forth on this continent, a new nation, conceived in Liberty, and dedicated to the proposition that all men are created equal."

Abraham Lincoln is among history's most revered individuals, renowned not only for holding a nation together during its greatest crisis but for the eloquence and brilliance of the many speeches he delivered. The most famous and most often quoted of these is his Gettysburg Address, a speech that historian and Lincoln scholar James McPherson has called "the world's foremost statement of freedom and democracy." For almost ninety years, Lincoln scholars lamented the fact that at a time when Abraham Lincoln was photographers' favorite subject, not a single photograph of Lincoln at Gettysburg had ever been found.

Then, in 1952, Josephine Cobb, chief of the Still Pictures Branch of the National Archives, made a startling discovery. About to retire, she was cleaning out her files when she came upon a previously overlooked glass photographic negative from the Archives' Civil War collection. The partially broken plate showed a huge crowd with top-hatted marshals standing in the background. Where else but at the Gettysburg cemetery dedication, where Lincoln delivered his historic speech, could such a large crowd overseen by marshals have gathered during the Civil War? Cobb exclaimed to herself.

With great anticipation, Cobb took the plate to the Archives' photographic laboratory, where she asked that the center portion of the image be enlarged. She became truly excited when this section disclosed that seated among the crowd in that area of the photograph were Governor Andrew Curtin of Pennsylvania and his young son, who, Cobb knew, had attended the Gettysburg Address.

With baited breath, Cobb then asked that the part of the scene toward which the Curtins and the others in the crowd were looking be enlarged. And there he was! President Abraham Lincoln, seated and hatless, captured by an unknown cameraman several hours, according to Cobb's estimation, before he mounted the platform and delivered a speech that will never be forgotten.

This is the photo found by Josephine Cobb, shown in its entirety.

Opposite: The larger view shows Governor Curtin and his son, and the inset reveals Lincoln before his legendary speech.

> *"Every man is said to have his peculiar ambition. . . . I can say for one that I have no other so great as that of being truly esteemed of my fellow men, by rendering myself worthy of their esteem."*

The Gettysburg photograph was a significant discovery. It is particularly important because of the vital role that photographs played in Abraham Lincoln's life. Before his days were over, photographs, even more than words, would not only reveal much about him but would help shape his destiny.

When photography first burst upon the scene in 1839, it was regarded as a miracle. Never before had it been possible to record things exactly as they were. Most important, human likenesses could be recorded. Unlike those drawn by artists, the new photographic portraits were exact replicas of the person sitting before the camera. And, for the first time, people from all walks of life could have their pictures recorded for posterity. Before photography, commissioning an artist to draw a portrait was very expensive and only the wealthy could afford it. Now, with the relatively inexpensive photographic process, almost anyone could have a portrait taken. Exact likenesses of the leading figures of the day could also be captured, giving people their first authentic views of those they had only read about or seen in artists' interpretations.

The first form of photography was known as the daguerreotype, named for Louis-Jacques-Mandé Daguerre, the French inventor who first captured a permanent photographic image. The image in a daguerreotype was captured on a mirrorlike silver or silver-plated copper plate and could not be copied. The daguerreotype on the facing page is the first photograph ever made of Abraham Lincoln, taken shortly after the thirty-seven-year-old had been elected to the Illinois House of Representatives. As he sat before Nicholas H. Shepherd's camera and became part of the very first generation of human beings ever to be photographed, Abraham Lincoln had no idea how important photography would be to his life and his career.

This self-portrait, taken by Robert Cornelius in 1839, is the earliest surviving American photograph.

Opposite: When Abraham Lincoln sat before Nicholas H. Shepherd's camera in 1846, he had no idea that in little more than a decade, he would become photographers' most sought-after human subject.

"I claim not to have controlled events, but confess plainly that events have controlled me."

During his lifetime, more photographs would be taken of Abraham Lincoln than any other person. And the man who took the most photographs of Lincoln was Mathew B. Brady, who became America's premier photographer. Brady's reputation as a photographer skyrocketed when he opened a gallery in Washington, featuring his Illustrious Americans exhibition. It was in this gallery that many of Brady's earliest photographs of Lincoln were displayed.

The careers of Abraham Lincoln and Mathew B. Brady became even more intertwined when, in 1860, Lincoln was nominated for the presidency. During the campaign, Brady took more than thirty-five photographs of the candidate, including one that Lincoln openly credited with winning him the election.

By the time the Civil War erupted, photography had advanced well beyond the simple daguerreotype. Although they could still not capture motion with their cameras, photographers could now produce pictures that could be printed and reprinted as many times as the photographer and the public desired. As soon as the conflict began, Brady set a new goal for himself—to become America's first battlefield photographer. Receiving permission from Lincoln himself, Brady organized and trained a team of talented and courageous photographers, most notably Alexander Gardner, and sent them throughout the war zones. The result would be an unprecedented photographic compilation of a nation at war with itself.

The Civil War would be waged throughout Lincoln's entire presidency. And Brady would continue to capture images of the man whose career he helped enhance. However, it would be his protégé Alexander Gardner who, during this period, would capture the two most remarkable Lincoln photographs of all.

Mathew B. Brady (standing beside the tree) looks on as one of his assistants captures a photograph of Union soldiers.

Opposite: Many of the pictures in this composite of sixty Lincoln portraits, including some drawings based on photographs, were taken by Mathew B. Brady or by one of his assistants, most notably Alexander Gardner and Timothy O'Sullivan.

J. FRANK ALDRICH

Posing with a Purpose

"If any personal description of me is thought desirable, it may be said, I am, in height, six feet, four inches, nearly; lean in flesh, weighing on an average one hundred and eighty pounds; dark complexion, with coarse black hair, and grey eyes—no other marks or brands recollected."

By the time Abraham Lincoln reached the White House, he had learned to use photographers and their cameras to his own advantage. It was a tactic that he had actually employed early on. At the beginning of his political career he had often deliberately mussed his hair before allowing his photographic portrait to be taken, so that the folks from the frontier who saw the picture would understand he was one of them. Even after he became a prosperous country lawyer and could afford the fanciest of clothes, Lincoln avoided wearing the frilly shirts and waistcoats popular in his day and presented himself to the camera as what he was—a true man of the people.

During the Civil War, he developed another strategy. Often at odds with his generals and other officers, who frequently ignored his orders, Lincoln would make certain that when asked to pose with them, or any other group for that matter, he stood in the center of the group, dominating the picture by drawing viewers' eyes to him and letting them know he was in command. Lincoln also accentuated his authority by wearing his tall stovepipe hat, which added to his six-foot, four-inch frame, enabling him to tower over those with whom he posed.

From the time, in 1857, that Alexander Hesler took this tousle-haired picture, Abraham Lincoln regarded it as perhaps his favorite of all the photographs taken of him.

Opposite: Abraham Lincoln posing with Union officers on the battlefield at Antietam.

> *"My best friend is the man who'll get me a book I ain't read."*

Abraham Lincoln, the man who would become the most photographed person of his day, began his life in the most humble surroundings. A true son of the frontier, he was born on February 12, 1809, in a one-room log cabin in Nolin Creek, Kentucky, and was named for his grandfather who had been killed by Indians. Neither his father, Thomas, nor his mother, Nancy, could read or write, but they were honest and hardworking people. Money was scarce and life was not easy, but they were determined to better themselves and their children's lives.

When Lincoln was seven, his father moved the family to Indiana, partly because he was disturbed by the growing presence of slavery in Kentucky and partly because making a living was becoming increasingly difficult. There, the young Lincoln became involved in the long hours of hard work that were required of every member of a farm family, which left so little time for school that Lincoln later stated all of his schooling amounted to less than one year.

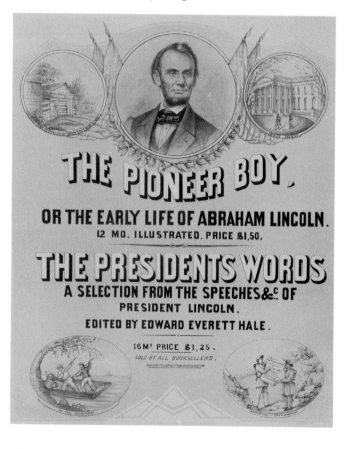

But no amount of work could put a damper on his love of knowledge and his insatiable curiosity about everything. Most of all, he was in love with books. His cousin Dennis Hanks said, "I never saw Abe after he was twelve that he didn't have a book in his hand or pocket." Throughout his life, he would walk almost any distance to get his hands on a book he felt he needed to read—even walking nearly twenty miles once to borrow a book from a lawyer named John Pitcher. This passion, along with his honesty and compassion for others, would determine who he was and who he was to become.

Abraham Lincoln's passion for reading would lead to his love of language and his ability to express himself in words that would echo throughout the world.

Opposite: Since there are no photographs of Lincoln's early life, this historical painting shows a young Lincoln reading a book by the light of the fireplace in his family's log cabin—one of his favorite boyhood activities.

An Unusual Young Man

"I am never easy . . . when I am handling a thought, till I have bounded it north and bounded it south, and bounded it east and bounded it west."

On at least two occasions, Abraham Lincoln almost did not survive his childhood. When he was ten, he was kicked in the head by a horse. Less than a year later, he fell in a rapidly rushing creek and almost drowned, but a neighborhood boy pulled him out of the water.

Lincoln was boisterous and he loved to play pranks. But even before the devastating experience of watching his mother pass away when he was only nine, he had displayed an uncommon concern for the pain and suffering of others, even the smallest animals. Later, stories of his tenderheartedness would sometimes be exaggerated, but it was Lincoln himself who wrote of how, after killing a wild turkey when he was eight, he felt such guilt that he never hunted or shot game again. And it was a boyhood friend who told the story of how Lincoln, after passing by a pig that was hopelessly stuck in mud, suddenly stopped, walked back almost a mile, and rescued the animal, not, recalled the friend, because Lincoln had a fondness for the pig but "just to take a pain out of his own mind."

By the time he was fifteen, Lincoln had grown to more than six feet tall. "The gangliest awkwardest feller, he appeared to be all joints," a neighbor remembered. But his years of hard labor had made him incredibly strong. Soon, stories of the young man's physical prowess spread throughout the county.

There were stories of how he had single-handedly picked up a 600-pound chicken coop and placed it on its new foundation; tales of how no one could come close to beating him at wrestling. Most of the stories were about his accomplishments with an ax. "My, how he could chop," a friend recalled. "If you heard him felling trees in a clearing, you would say that there were three men at work."

In his own county, Abraham Lincoln was becoming a legend. Before his life and career were over, he would become one of the nation's most legendary figures.

Abraham Lincoln posing beside a bust of George Washington. Throughout Lincoln's presidency, many artists created paintings suggesting that Lincoln was attaining a status previously reserved solely for the nation's first president.

Opposite: In this painting, Norman Rockwell depicted Abraham Lincoln with two of the objects that were his constant companions throughout his early years—a book and an ax.

A Turning Point

"This is a world of compensations; and he who would be no slave, must consent to have no slave."

By the time he was twenty, Lincoln had grown restless. There was so much of the nation, and he had seen none of it. Then a local merchant, impressed with the young man's strength and character, hired him to take a flatboat loaded with farm produce on a 1,200-mile journey down the Mississippi River to New Orleans.

Lincoln was thrilled by the prospect of visiting his first genuine city. Although he was fascinated with the sight of the towering sailing vessels that jammed New Orleans Harbor and with the crowds of people from around the world that filled the city's streets, he was shocked at something else he witnessed.

More than 200 slave dealers conducted their business in New Orleans, and Lincoln was horrified at the sight of gangs of men, women, and children shackled in chains, being prodded along to the auction blocks to be sold off like horses or cattle. It was his first encounter with slavery, and it was a crucial turning point in his life. Although he did not realize it at the time, his political career, first as a candidate for Congress and the presidency, and then as president, would be dominated and shaped by his feelings concerning what he regarded as "that evil institution."

Articulating his strongest feelings, he would exclaim, "Whenever [I] hear any one arguing for slavery I feel a strong impulse to see it tried on him personally."

To Abraham Lincoln, slavery struck at the very foundations of the country he loved. "As I would not be a *slave*," he would state, "so I would not be a *master*. This expresses my idea of democracy." His lifelong struggle against slavery began in New Orleans.

New Orleans at approximately the time that Abraham Lincoln visited the city and encountered the evils of slavery.

Opposite: An early photograph of a slave family. His encounters with slavery would lead Abraham Lincoln to state, "If slavery is not wrong, nothing is wrong."

False Starts

When Lincoln returned from New Orleans, his friend Dennis Offett offered him a job running his general store in New Salem, Illinois. Before long, folks began coming into the store just to hear Lincoln's humorous stories and tall tales. In 1832, however, Offett was forced to close his store. For Dennis Offett it was a setback. For Abraham Lincoln it was the beginning of a political career. Even before the store had failed, Lincoln's friends had been urging him to run for the Illinois state legislature.

Just as Lincoln was ready to start campaigning, however, a Native American chief and his men crossed the Mississippi, intending to take back their land. Lincoln immediately answered a call for state militia and was elected captain of his unit. By the time he returned home, he had little time to campaign outside his home district, where folks knew and admired him, and was defeated.

He had not only lost his first election, but he was once again unemployed. After an unsuccessful attempt at running his own general store, he took on a variety of jobs—splitting fence rails, working at a grist mill, signing on as a surveyor's assistant. He even managed to get himself appointed as New Salem's postmaster.

The job of postmaster turned out to be another turning point in Lincoln's life. The postmaster delivered newspapers to subscribers along with the mail. This gave Lincoln the opportunity to read through the nation's papers before delivering them, acquainting him with the national events and political developments of the day.

In 1834, Lincoln decided to make a second try for the Illinois state legislature. This time he won. Wearing the first suit he ever owned, he set out for Vandalia, which was then the Illinois state capital. It was there that fate stepped in in the form of another young legislator, named John Todd Stuart.

This rare daguerreotype is the first photograph ever taken showing a surveyor and his equipment.

Opposite: This photograph shows a replica of the type of New Salem log building in which Abraham Lincoln tended store, served as postmaster, and launched his political career.

Birth of a Lawyer

"Resolve to be honest at all events; and if in your own judgment you cannot be an honest lawyer, resolve to be honest without being a lawyer."

John Todd Stuart was already making a name for himself as an attorney, and as he and Lincoln struck up a friendship, he began urging Lincoln to become a lawyer himself. Nothing would have pleased Lincoln more. Back in Indiana, Lincoln had discovered something that truly fascinated him. In those days, frontier courts did not hold regular sessions but met on a specially designated series of days. Lawyers from throughout the wide county would travel to courts to plead their cases, attracting hundreds of spectators and creating a circuslike atmosphere.

Whenever he could, Lincoln attended these sessions, where he watched and listened in awe as the lawyers put forth their arguments to the accompaniment of raucous shouts of approval or disapproval from the spectators. To Lincoln, however, it was much more than mere entertainment. As he listened, he gained a profound respect for the law and for those who interpreted and defended it. Given his lack of formal education, he could never imagine himself having such an opportunity.

Then Stuart told him that very few practicing attorneys had attended law school. They had become lawyers simply by studying the law, usually under the supervision of a practicing attorney, until they had read enough to demonstrate an adequate knowledge of legal principles.

For the next three years, a period in which he was twice reelected to the state legislature, Lincoln pored through every law book he could obtain. On March 1, 1837, after appearing before the clerk of the Illinois State Supreme Court and demonstrating his legal knowledge, Abraham Lincoln received his license to practice law. And he had more than just the license. John Stuart offered him a job as his junior partner in Stuart's law office in Springfield, a position that Lincoln happily accepted.

It was in frontier courthouses such as this one in Paris, Illinois, that Abraham Lincoln first gained his fascination with the law and the legal profession.

Opposite: This daguerreotype, taken in Beardstown, Illinois, in 1857, shows a forty-eight-year-old Abraham Lincoln dressed in the white suit he often wore while pleading the cases that made him one of his region's most successful and prosperous lawyers.

> *"Whatever woman may cast her lot with mine, should any ever do so, it is my intention to do all in my power to make her happy and contented; and there is nothing I can immagine (sic), that would make me more unhappy than to fail in the effort."*

By the time Lincoln rode into Springfield, it had become the Illinois state capital. But Springfield was still a small town of 1,500 people. The railroad had not yet reached it; the only roads leading into it were really paths made by the covered wagons. There were no paved streets, no sidewalks, no streetlights.

But Lincoln was delighted to be there, and he was now busier than he had ever been in his life. There was much to be learned from John Todd Stuart about the practical side of being a lawyer. In the meantime, in 1838 and again in 1840, he was reelected to the state legislature, an accomplishment that did not surprise his friends or colleagues. What did shock them, however, was that Abraham Lincoln fell in love.

Her name was Mary Todd and theirs was a most unusual match. Born in Kentucky to slaveholding parents, Mary Todd, a cousin of John Todd Stuart, was highly educated, spoke French fluently, recited poetry, and traveled in the highest Springfield society. But she saw something in the rough-hewn country lawyer and politician. Even more than he, she was convinced that he was destined to go far. It was a stormy, on-again, off-again courtship, but on November 4, 1842, they were married.

Two years later, now with a wife and one-year-old son, Robert, to support, Lincoln left Stuart, opened his own law firm, and invited a young attorney named William Herndon to join him as his junior partner. Herndon was skilled at the time-consuming research necessary in the preparation of a legal case, which freed Lincoln to concentrate on the far more exciting task of trying the case itself. And in 1846, Herndon's presence became even more important, when Lincoln was elected to the U.S. Congress. Leaving his junior partner behind to run the office, Lincoln and his family headed to Washington.

Throughout much of Lincoln's life, the technology did not exist to allow photographs to be printed in books, newspapers, or magazines. The pictures of Lincoln that appeared in these publications were commonly copied from photographs.

Opposite: Abraham Lincoln, the man who loved to laugh, is never seen smiling because the long exposure time made it impossible for a subject to hold a smile long enough for the picture to be completed. This photograph of Lincoln became the image used on the U.S. five-dollar bill.

Mary Todd Lincoln

"My wife is as handsome as when she was a girl, and I, a poor nobody then, fell in love with her, and what is more, I have never fallen out."

No other president had ever been forced to endure as many burdens as Abraham Lincoln. It was a fate that extended beyond issues such as slavery and war into Lincoln's personal life as well. Among these personal challenges were those presented by the character and actions of the woman to whom he was married.

As president, Lincoln's necessary preoccupation with the affairs of the nation, and particularly the Civil War, forced him to spend hours, even days away from his wife, a fact that Mary Todd Lincoln simply could not handle. Losing control, she began verbally abusing trusted White House servants. Then she undertook a lavish renovation of the White House, which cost so much that even her husband's greatest supporters were appalled about the thousands of dollars being spent on china, silverware, chandeliers, and carpets when the Union soldiers in the field "cannot have enough blankets." Not only did Mrs. Lincoln ignore the criticisms that followed but she extended her shopping sprees to include personal items, filling her closets and trunks with more clothing, jewelry, and other items than she could possibly wear.

Through it all, Abraham Lincoln tolerated his wife's extravagance and extremes of mood with an indulgence well beyond that of most mortals. To a friend who had just witnessed one of Mary Todd Lincoln's irrational outbursts of temper, Lincoln stated, "It does her lots of good and doesn't hurt me a bit." And to a farmer who had complained to the president about the verbal abuse he had taken from Mrs. Lincoln, who mistakenly thought she had been sold bad produce, Lincoln replied, "My friend, I regret to hear this, but let me ask you in all candor, can't you endure for a few moments what I have had as my daily portion for the last fifteen years?"

Mary Todd Lincoln around the time Lincoln met and fell in love with her.

Opposite: This photograph of Mary Todd Lincoln, taken at the time her husband occupied the White House, shows her in one of the lavish gowns she loved to wear.

Lincoln's Sorrow

"I am now the most miserable man living. If what I feel were equally distributed to the whole human family, there would not be one cheerful face on the earth."

Abraham Lincoln had four children and, as with so many other things in his life, along with the joy they brought him, there was deep sorrow attached. All of Lincoln's children were born in Springfield, but only Robert, his firstborn, lived to adulthood. Successful as both a lawyer and a businessman, Robert also provided important service to the nation, serving as secretary of war under Presidents James Garfield and Chester Arthur and as minister to Great Britain under President Benjamin Harrison.

Tragically, Lincoln's second son, Edward, was not yet four years old when he died of tuberculosis. The brief life of Lincoln's third son, Willie, was also marked by tragedy. He was only eleven when he was stricken by typhoid fever, possibly from drinking contaminated water, and died in the White House.

Thomas "Tad" Lincoln, born in 1853, was the most fun loving and mischievous of all the Lincoln children and was a particular favorite of his father. While living in the White House, Tad continually caused mischief, such as ringing the bells in the attic, interrupting cabinet meetings, and offering tours of the

executive mansion for a fee. An indulgent parent, Lincoln took great delight in Tad's pranks. But, like Edward and Willie, Tad died at a young age. In May 1871, while returning home from Europe with his mother, eighteen-year-old Tad caught a shipboard fever and became seriously ill. Two months later, after he was further weakened by tuberculosis, Tad passed away. More than six years after the sixteenth president's own violent death, tragedy continued to haunt the Lincoln family.

Robert Lincoln (top) sat for this photograph shortly after he returned from serving with distinction as a Union officer in the Civil War.

Willie Lincoln (bottom), age six, in a photograph taken before the family left Springfield for Washington DC.

Opposite (top): Abraham Lincoln with his son Tad.

Opposite (bottom): A rare daguerreotype of Edward Lincoln.

Disappointment

"I have never had a feeling politically that did not spring from the sentiments embodied in the Declaration of Independence."

Family tragedy was still ahead of him when Abraham Lincoln, with great anticipation, took his seat in the U.S. House of Representatives. As a newcomer, he soon discovered he would not be involved in any major legislative activities. He became bored by being forced to listen to long hours of debate over what, to him, were trivial issues. And Mary had disliked Washington so much that she moved back to Springfield with the young Robert and the newborn Edward. With his family gone, Lincoln grew depressed. When his two-year term was completed, he decided to return to Springfield and throw himself fully into the law.

He began to participate in that unique type of county lawyering that had fascinated him back in Indiana. Twice a year a judge rode the 500-mile circuit, holding court in each of the dozens of far-flung county seats. He was followed by a band of lawyers who picked up clients along the way. It was an arduous undertaking, but Lincoln loved it, particularly because it gave him a chance to meet face-to-face with ordinary people, to visit their homes, and to talk to them about everything from their farming methods to their political leanings.

And as he talked with those he met on his travels and pored through the newspapers back in his law office, he could not help but be aware that the nation was heading toward one of the most serious crises it had ever faced. The number of slaves in the South had grown to more than three million.

Lincoln despised slavery. But his personal feelings were tempered by a practical reality. He was convinced that

the efforts of those who were demanding that Southerners give up their slaves would inevitably lead to splitting the nation apart. The answer, he believed, lay in making certain that slavery was not permitted outside the states where it already existed, specifically in each new state as it came into the Union. He was certain that if Congress made sure that slavery was contained where it was, it would eventually die "a natural death."

Abraham Lincoln's Springfield law office, which he shared with William Herndon. The artist exaggerated the size and neatness of the room, which, in the words of one newspaper, was "the most untidy law-office in the United States."

Opposite: An early photograph of the U.S. House of Representatives. In this chamber many decisions would be made that would affect Abraham Lincoln's political career.

A House Divided

"I would rather be defeated with this expression ['a house divided against itself cannot stand']... than be victorious without it."

Abraham Lincoln was stunned when, in 1857, the U.S. Supreme Court handed down a decision declaring that Congress did not have the power to prohibit slavery in any of the nation's territories. The ruling led him to reenter politics and do what he could to keep the nation from splitting apart.

By this time, his circuit-riding travels throughout Illinois and his reputation for honesty and eloquence had made his name known throughout the state. In early 1858, when he announced his candidacy for the U.S. Senate, Lincoln received so much support that, at the party's nominating convention in June, the 1,200 delegates unanimously passed a resolution naming him their candidate.

On the evening of his nomination, Lincoln delivered an acceptance speech that, in its very first paragraph, put the issue of slavery directly before the American people. "A house divided against itself cannot stand," Lincoln proclaimed. "I believe this government cannot endure, permanently half *slave* and half *free*. I do not expect the Union to be dissolved—I do not expect the house to *fall*—but I *do* expect it will cease to be divided. It will become *all* one thing, or *all* the other." The speech would awaken the entire nation to the unprecedented crisis it now faced. It would forever be known as the "House Divided Speech," the first of other orations to follow that would make both the words and the man who spoke them immortal.

Lincoln's speech was greeted with alarm in the South by those who interpreted it as a direct attack on slavery. Many in his own party worried aloud that it had been too radical and had jeopardized Lincoln's chances for election. To them Lincoln replied, "You will see the day when you will consider it the wisest thing I ever said."

Settlers arriving in covered wagons brought with them the explosive issue of whether slavery would be permitted in the territories when they were admitted as states.

Opposite: This illustration from a widely distributed broadside was one of the most powerful weapons used by the abolitionists in their campaign against slavery.

The Great Debates

"Though I now sink out of view, and shall be forgotten, I believe I have made some marks which will tell for the cause of civil liberty long after I am gone."

The "House Divided Speech" set the stage for arguably the most remarkable political campaign in U.S. history. Throughout the summer of 1858, Lincoln and his opponent, Stephen A. Douglas, engaged in seven three-hour debates that have been described as "the greatest public oratory in the nation's history."

The two men attracted the largest political audiences the nation had ever known. Their words echoed throughout the country, printed in newspapers in every state and territory. And no wonder. What they stated represented the clearest and most articulate evidence yet presented of how far the two sections of the nation had drifted apart. Stating that he believed the nation *could* endure half slave and half free, Douglas proclaimed, "I am opposed to Negro citizenship in any and every form. . . . I believe [this government] was made by white men for the benefit of white men." Responding to Douglas's remarks, Lincoln proclaimed, slavery was a moral issue that was a blot on the entire nation. "There is no reason in the world why the Negro is not entitled to all the natural rights enumerated in the Declaration of Independence," stated Lincoln, "the right to life, liberty and the pursuit of happiness. I hold that he is as much entitled to these as the white man."

When the debates were finally over, the entire nation, not just the people of Illinois, anxiously awaited the election results. At the time, U.S. senators were elected by the state legislators. And when the votes were counted, the Republicans had not won enough seats in the legislature—so Lincoln was defeated by a narrow margin. For the man who had poured his heart and soul into the campaign, it was a bitter disappointment. He is quoted as saying, "I feel like the boy who stubbed his toe. I am too big to cry and too badly hurt to laugh."

This cartoonist depicted the Lincoln-Douglas debates as a prize fight, with the winner, in his opinion, having a clear path to the White House.

Opposite: Although he was short in stature, Stephen A. Douglas was considered a giant in politics. After winning the Senate election over Lincoln, he went on to become the leading figure in Congress.

"Nearly all men can stand adversity, but if you want to test a man's character, give him power."

What Lincoln did not realize was that his performance in his debates with Douglas had greatly impressed tens of thousands of citizens and particularly Republican Party leaders. Within weeks of the senatorial election, some of these leaders began mentioning him as a possible candidate for the presidential election of 1860. Asked what he thought about that, Lincoln replied, ". . . the taste is in my mouth a little."

On May 16, 1860, Republican delegates from throughout the nation gathered in an enormous new convention hall in Chicago nicknamed the "Wigwam." Their task was to select the man who would be the party's candidate in the presidential election to be held in November. As the boisterous three-day convention began, two men, William Seward and Salmon P. Chase, were the definite front-runners. Although he was a decided underdog, Lincoln's name had also become bandied about by many of the delegates.

When the first vote was taken, Seward, as most expected, surged far ahead. But with 233 votes needed for victory, he was still 60 votes short of the nomination. And there had been a gigantic surprise. Lincoln had received 102 votes, far more than Salmon Chase had. On the second ballot, in which Seward again fell short, Lincoln picked up even more votes. Now an increasing number of delegates, anxious to back a winner, jumped off the Seward bandwagon. When the third ballot was taken, Abraham Lincoln tallied 132 more votes than was needed for nomination. The man who only twelve years earlier had grown tired of politics forever had become the Republican Party's candidate for president of the United States.

After Abraham Lincoln was elected president, he named to his cabinet several of those who had been favored above him to win the presidential nomination. As shown in this illustration, clockwise from the top, they included William Seward, Secretary of State; Gideon Welles, Secretary of the Navy; Salmon Chase, Secretary of the Treasury; and Edwin Stanton, Secretary of War.

Opposite: This political illustration of "the prominent candidates" for the Republican Party presidential nomination featured William Seward as the leading candidate. Abraham Lincoln was pictured at the bottom of the illustration, along with others "unlikely to gain the nomination."

PROMINENT CANDIDATES FOR THE REPUBLICAN PRESIDENTIAL NOMINATION AT CHICAGO.—[From Photographs by Brady.]

"My friends—No one, not in my situation, can appreciate my feeling of sadness at this parting. To this place, and the kindness of these people, I owe every thing."

Nowhere was Lincoln's nomination for president greeted with greater joy than in Springfield, where he was so admired. The photographer who captured this image recorded one of the main events of the celebration, a giant parade that took eight hours to pass by Lincoln's home. In the photograph, Lincoln, clad in a white suit, stands at the right of the doorway. Mary Todd Lincoln, wearing a bonnet, peeks out of the far left downstairs window. Staring out of the second window from the left on the second floor is young Willie Lincoln. Thirty-three young women ride in the portion of the parade shown, each representing one of the nation's states, followed by "Kansas"—hoping to become the thirty-fourth—carrying a sign pleading, "Won't you let me in."

Mary

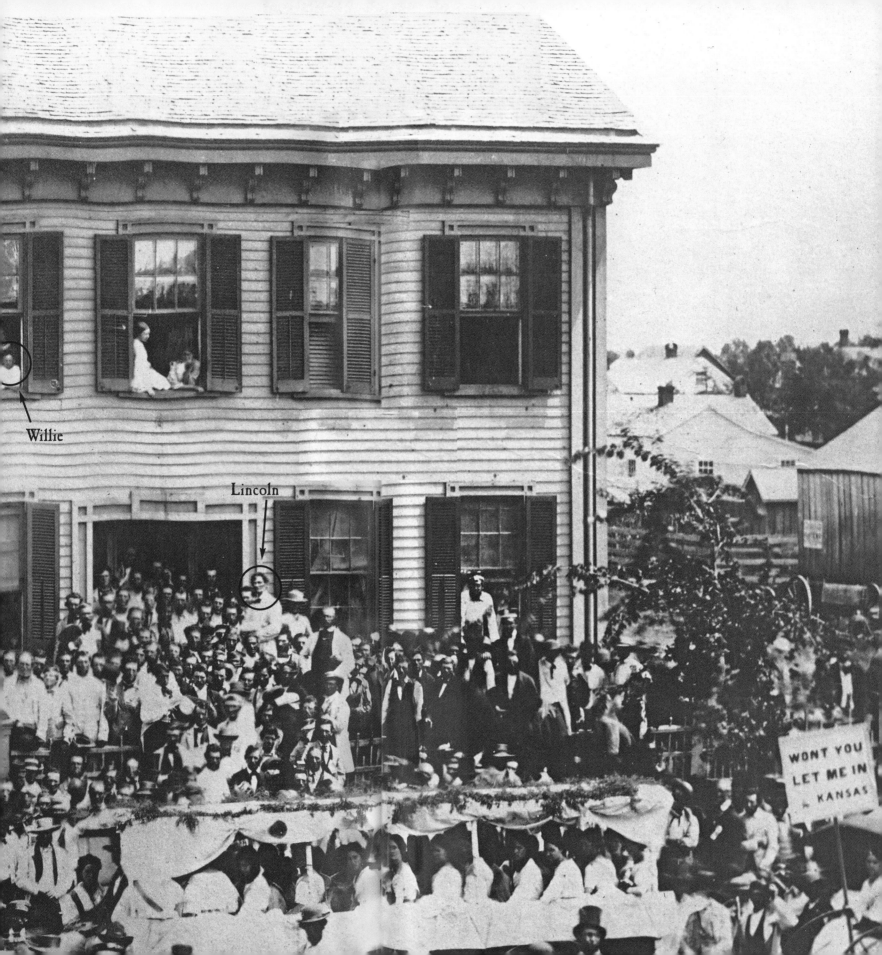

Willie

Lincoln

WONT YOU
LET ME IN
KANSAS

"*Let us have faith that right makes might, and in that faith, let us, to the end, dare to do our duty as we understand it.*"

As the 1860 presidential campaign began, Lincoln's opponents attacked him mercilessly, portraying him as "a country bumpkin," a man unfit to be president. Then Lincoln received an invitation to deliver a major speech in New York City before some of the most powerful and knowledgeable individuals in the nation. Its importance was not lost on Lincoln. This, he knew, was to be no backwoods address to frontier farmers.

Lincoln had carefully crafted the address in three parts. In the first part he explained the Republican Party's belief that the federal government should prohibit slavery in the national territories was neither new nor revolutionary. In the second part of the speech, aimed at calming the fears of those in the South, Lincoln declared emphatically that the Republican Party posed no threat to slavery where it already existed.

He saved his most forceful words for the final section of the address, remarks directly intended for his fellow Northerners. They must, he told them, persist in excluding slavery from spreading into the national territories and confine it to the states where it already existed.

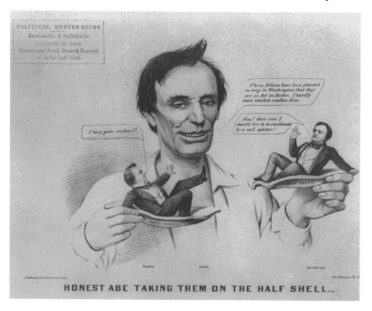

HONEST ABE TAKING THEM ON THE HALF SHELL..

No one had expected so straightforward, so intelligent, and so eloquent an orator. As one, the audience that filled the hall of the Cooper Union Institute stood in loud and prolonged applause. One eyewitness summed up the entire evening's experience. "When Lincoln rose to speak," he wrote, "I was greatly disappointed. . . . I had, for an instant, a feeling of pity for so ungainly a man. . . . But pretty soon he began to get into his subject; . . . his face lighted as with an inward fire; the whole man was transfigured. . . . When I came out of the hall, . . . a friend, with his eyes aglow, asked me what I thought of Abe Lincoln, the rail-splitter. I said: 'He's the greatest man since St. Paul.' And I think so yet."

This caricature of Abraham Lincoln, drawn as the 1860 presidential campaign began, was typical of the many in which he was portrayed in an unflattering manner.

Opposite: New York City around the time that Abraham Lincoln arrived to deliver his Cooper Union speech.

> *"I have stepped out upon this platform that I may see you and that you may see me, and in the arrangement I have the best of the bargain."*

Several hours before he gave his Cooper Union speech, Lincoln went to Mathew B. Brady's studio to have his photograph taken. Brady was aware that his task was to make the man, who had so often been portrayed by his opponents as unfit for the nation's highest office, look presidential. Brady began by emphasizing the candidate's great height, telling Lincoln that, rather than photographing him sitting down as Brady and other photographers had previously done, he was going to photograph him standing up. Then, in order to hide Lincoln's scrawny neck, Brady pulled Lincoln's shirt collar up as high as it would go. Brady also added props to the picture that he felt would enhance Lincoln's image. Behind Lincoln's right shoulder he placed the model of a pillar, long a symbol of strength. To Lincoln's left, he placed a pile of books, suggesting learning and the quest for knowledge.

The speech Lincoln gave at Cooper Union that night won over scores of influential New York politicians and civic leaders. The photograph, which was widely circulated, changed the minds of even a greater number of voters. When the election was over, Abraham Lincoln publicly stated, "Brady and the Cooper Union Institute made me president."

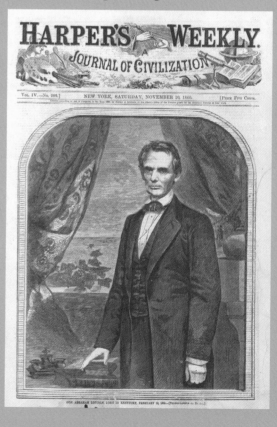

Newspapers and magazines were quick to print illustrations based on Mathew B. Brady's Cooper Union photograph. This illustration adorned the cover of *Harper's Weekly*, the nation's most widely read publication.

Opposite: Mathew B. Brady's photograph that Lincoln credited with having won him the White House.

"Sir, my concern is not whether God is on our side. My great concern is to be on God's side."

On **November 6, 1860,** a bitterly divided nation went to the polls and elected Abraham Lincoln president of the United States. His victory was based totally on the support he received in the North. Nine states in the South had refused even to put his name on the ballot.

Then on December 24, 1860, three months before his inauguration, the state of South Carolina seceded from the Union. By February 9, 1861, six other Southern states—Mississippi, Florida, Alabama, Georgia, Louisiana, and Texas—had joined South Carolina and had formed the Confederate States of America, an independent nation dedicated to the preservation of slavery.

On February 11, 1861, Lincoln, accompanied by his family, friends, and advisors, boarded a special train in Springfield and set out for Washington. The journey to the nation's capital took twelve days. But before it was over, it had become the most unusual journey any president-elect had ever taken. As the train approached Cincinnati, a loaded grenade was discovered in a small carpetbag in the presidential car. By the time the train reached New York, a local newspaper was reporting that "large rewards have been offered in the cotton states to whoever would take [Lincoln's] life before [inauguration day]." And as the train approached Baltimore, reports circulated that 15,000 men were planning to blow up the railroad tracks and set fire to the train.

The threat never materialized, but as a result, Lincoln was literally smuggled into Washington in disguise. After riding through the night in a small, unmarked railroad car, he was given an old, long coat to wear along with a wide-brimmed farmer's hat, which he could pull down over his face. And under the cover of darkness the man who was to be the sixteenth president of the United States entered the nation's capital.

Washington DC, at the time Abraham Lincoln was elected president. Featured prominently is Alexander Gardner's photographic gallery and studio, where Lincoln had several presidential portraits taken.

Opposite: This is the only photograph taken of Abraham Lincoln as he made his way from Springfield to Washington for his inauguration. Lincoln is shown at an appearance at Philadelphia's Independence Hall. Tad Lincoln can be seen leaning on the railing, just above the flag's star at the right.

Lincoln

Tad

Lincoln's Beard

"As to the whiskers, having never worn any, do you not think people would call it a piece of silly affectation if I were to begin it now?"

Thanks to the medium of photography, those who viewed pictures of Abraham Lincoln taken shortly before the 1860 presidential election encountered a man who looked quite different from the person who had received his party's nomination. In an age when it was becoming increasingly fashionable for men to wear whiskers, Lincoln had always been clean shaven. But less than a month before the election he received a touching letter from an eleven-year-old Westfield, New York, girl. Her name was Grace Bedell, and in her letter she wrote, "My father has just [come] home from the fair and brought home your picture. . . . I have got 4 brothers and part of them will vote for you any way and if you let your whiskers grow I will try to get the rest of them to vote for you. You would look a great deal better for your face is so thin. All the ladies like whiskers and they would tease their husbands to vote for you and then you would be President. . . ."

Young Grace's letter reached Lincoln at a most interesting time since only three days earlier a group of influential New York Republicans had written to him also suggesting that he would look better in whiskers. Whether it was through the urging of a charming eleven-year-old or that of much older Republican Party members, Lincoln took the advice and began growing the beard that would be one of his most distinguishing features for the rest of his life.

By late 1861, when Mathew B. Brady captured this image, Lincoln had grown the full beard that would remain with him the rest of his life.

Opposite (top): Abraham Lincoln's final beardless photograph was taken by Illinois photographer T. Painter Pearson early in November 1860.

Opposite (bottom): This photograph, taken on November 25, 1860, by Chicago photographer Samuel Alschuler, was the first to show Lincoln sprouting a beard.

"I happen temporarily to occupy this big White House. I am living witness that any one of your children may look to come here as my father's child has."

As Abraham Lincoln stood on a platform above the Capitol steps, he knew he was about to make the most important inaugural speech that any incoming president had ever delivered. Somehow he had to keep together a nation that was already splitting apart.

First, Lincoln assured the Southern states that he had no intention of calling for the abolition of slavery in the states where it already existed, and he declared that his government had no intention of attacking the South. Then, Lincoln reminded both North and South of his faith in the wisdom of the people. "Why should there not be a patient confidence in the ultimate justice of the people? . . . We are not enemies," he exclaimed. "We must not be enemies. Though passion may [be] strained, it must not break our bonds of affection."

It was a heartfelt appeal, but the division between North and South had already grown too deep. Less than two weeks after Lincoln's inauguration, a crisis developed at the federal garrison in Charleston, South Carolina. When it seceded, South Carolina had claimed all federal property in the state. But federal troops still manned Fort Sumter.

Now South Carolina's governor was demanding that the troops be removed. The situation was made worse by the fact that the garrison was running out of supplies. Neither Lincoln nor his cabinet members was certain what to do. Finally, Lincoln ordered that a supply fleet be sent to the fort. On the morning of April 12, 1861, as the fleet approached Charleston, Confederate cannons that had been set up around the harbor began to bombard the fort. The first shots had been fired. The North and the South were at war.

There were no photographers present when the events at Fort Sumter took place. But artists were quick to present their depictions of the bombardment that signaled the beginning of the Civil War.

Opposite (left): James Buchanan, Lincoln's predecessor in the White House, whose soft stance on slavery helped shape Lincoln's position on the subject. Opposite (right): Hannibal Hamlin, Lincoln's first vice president, was later replaced by Southerner Andrew Johnson to help strengthen Lincoln's chance for reelection. Had Lincoln been assassinated six weeks earlier, Hamlin would have been our seventeenth president.

Children at War

"In this sad world of ours, sorrow comes to all; and, to the young, it comes with bitterest agony, because it takes them unawares."

The Civil War was unlike anything Americans had ever experienced, or even imagined. Before it was over, more than two million men would fight for the North, while close to one million would serve in the Confederate forces. More than three million would fight and more than 650,000 would die. They would be killed by bullets and cannonballs and explosions and a host of other weapons. But, at a time when doctors had no experience in dealing with battlefield casualties or widespread disease, more would die from inadequate treatment of their injuries or from diseases such as dysentery, measles, malaria, and typhoid than from their wounds.

The pictures taken by the Civil War photographers would reveal this horrific toll even more vividly than could have been accomplished in words. The photographs also revealed another startling fact. Tens of thousands of the soldiers and sailors were not men but children, many ten years old and younger.

Officially, children seventeen years and younger were not allowed in either army without their parents' permission. But the lure of adventure led both Northern and Southern youngsters, most unaware of the horrors of war, to run away from home and join the fighting by using false names. Union and Confederate military leaders, desperate for troops, commonly accepted the youngsters without question.

Before marching off to war, many of the soldiers in both armies visited daguerreotypists' studios, where they had their photograph taken to be sent home to the loved ones they had left behind. It was pictures like the one on the facing page of a ten-year-old "powder monkey" aboard the Union gunship USS *New Hampshire* that dramatically revealed how young even many of the combat soldiers were.

Many children in both the Union and Confederate armies served as drummer boys, who beat out such battlefield signals as "charge" or "retreat" during battles.

Opposite: This ten-year-old boy was a "powder monkey," the name given to the youngsters who served aboard Civil War gunships and who had the dangerous task of carrying live ammunition from belowdecks to the guns mounted above.

A Worthy Opponent

"When I think of the sacrifices of life yet to be offered and the hearts and homes yet to be made desolate before this dreadful war . . . is over, my heart is like lead within me, and I feel, at times, like hiding in deep darkness."

When the Civil War began, Union troops had marched off to battle, many confident of a quick and easy victory. But the early encounters with Southern forces brought nothing but defeat. Much of it was due to the skilled military leadership of Confederate commander Robert E. Lee.

On July 21, 1861, in the first significant battle of the conflict, Union troops were trounced at the small railroad town of Manassas Junction, Virginia, more commonly called Bull Run. In the spring of 1862, Lee followed up this initial victory by driving a much larger Union army of more than 100,000 men out of Virginia and back into Washington. Then, in early April 1862, at a Tennessee crossroads named Shiloh, a hoped-for Northern victory turned into a costly stalemate that left 3,000 men dead and 20,000 more either wounded or missing. In the White House, Lincoln hardly had time to comprehend the enormity of that carnage when he received news that Lee had scored yet another Confederate victory at the Second Battle of Bull Run.

For Lincoln, a man whose personality throughout his whole life had fluctuated between good-natured, sometimes raucous humor and sadness, the Civil War years would be the unhappiest time of all. After hearing of the thousands of men who had been killed during one battle, he clasped his hands behind his back, looked off into space, and cried out, "My God! My God! What will the country say?"

A large number of both Union and Confederate officers were graduates of the West Point Military Academy. This is a rare photograph of Academy cadets, taken at approximately the time that Robert E. Lee attended West Point.

Opposite: Robert E. Lee. As soon as the Civil War began, Abraham Lincoln offered Lee command of all Union troops. But Lee felt that his main loyalty was to his native Virginia and instead accepted command of all Confederate forces.

Lee Invades the North

"In coming to us, he tenders us an advantage which we should not waive. . . . As we must beat him somewhere, or fail finally, we can do it, if at all, easier near to us, than far away."

Flush with the victories he had gained on Southern soil, Lee now initiated the boldest move of the war thus far by launching an invasion of the North in the hope of perhaps even capturing Washington. He began by leading his army into Maryland, where he hoped to encourage the people in that border state to join the Confederacy. By September 16, 1862, Lee had positioned more than 40,000 troops on the hills above Antietam Creek near the village of Sharpsburg, Maryland. On the other side of the creek, Union general George McClellan had assembled more than twice that number of Union soldiers.

What followed on September 17 was, and still remains, the bloodiest single day in American history. When the dawn-to-darkness battle was over, nearly 25,000 of the 120,000 men who had taken part had been either killed

or wounded. Finally overwhelmed by the superior number of Union forces, Lee had no choice but to abandon his Northern invasion and order his weary troops to retreat back to Southern territory. McClellan, on the other hand, even though he still had twice as many men as Lee and a far greater number of cannons, rifles, and supplies, inexplicably decided not to pursue the enemy, though, had he done so, he might well have delivered a fatal blow to the Confederacy. When news of McClellan's failure to secure the total victory that seemed to be in his hands was telegraphed back to Lincoln, the president, who had long been frustrated by the commander's inability to act decisively, relayed a message to the general, stating, "If you don't want to use the army, I would like to borrow it for a while."

Abraham Lincoln meeting with one of his generals. Lincoln's frustration with the indecisiveness of his military commanders was a continual burden to him.

Opposite: It would not be until the Civil War was over that cameras were perfected to the point where they could capture movement. But somehow Alexander Gardner was able to take this image of the fighting at Antietam, the only action picture of the war.

Shocking a Nation

The Civil War was the first American armed conflict to be photographed. And it was through photographs that the American public was introduced to the horrors of war. Following each battle, it was standard practice for both sides to declare a truce so that they could bury their dead. The guns of Antietam had hardly ceased when members of Mathew B. Brady's photographic corps began taking pictures of the dead, the likes of which Americans had never seen. The photographs were then taken to Brady's New York gallery and studio, where, within a month of the battle, he mounted a display of many of the images.

Commenting on the exhibition, the *New York Times* declared that "Mr. Brady has done something to bring home to us the terrible reality and earnestness of war. . . . Crowds of people are constantly going up the stairs [to see the pictures]. Follow them and you will find them bending over photographic views of the fearful battlefield, taken immediately after the action. If [Brady] has not brought bodies and laid them in our dooryards and along streets, he has done something very like it." Poet Oliver Wendell Holmes, whose own son was badly wounded at Antietam, echoed these sentiments. "Let him who wants to know what war is, look at these [photographs]!" he exclaimed.

The capturing of images of fallen soldiers on both sides of the conflict would continue throughout the long war. Commenting on one image taken by fellow cameraman Timothy O'Sullivan, Alexander Gardner would write, "Slowly over the misty fields of Gettysburg . . . came the sunless morn after the retreat by Lee's broken army. Through the shadowy vapors, it was indeed a 'harvest of death' that was presented. . . . Such a picture conveys a useful moral: . . . Let them aid in preventing such another calamity falling upon the nation." Unfortunately, the pictures would not prevent other wars from taking place. But thanks to the Civil War photographs, Americans would never again march off so innocently to war.

This photograph of a dead Confederate sniper was taken by an unknown Civil War photographer after the Battle of Petersburg.

Opposite: Alexander Gardner, who took many of the photographs of the fallen on both sides of the conflict, characterized what he witnessed as "a harvest of death."

> *"I never, in my life, felt more certain that I was doing right, than I do in signing this paper."*

Lincoln was so angry with McClellan that he was ready to replace him with another general. But Lee's retreat and abandonment of his invasion of the North had been the first positive military news Lincoln had received. And he was convinced that it gave him a long-awaited opportunity.

When the South seceded, Lincoln knew his greatest concern had to be saving the Union, no matter what the cost. In August 1862, with the war news continually discouraging, he had disappointed abolitionist leaders by declaring, "My paramount object in this struggle is to save the Union, and it is not either to save or destroy slavery. If I could save the Union without freeing any slave I would do it; and if I could save it by freeing all the slaves I would do it; and if I could save it by freeing some and leaving others alone I would also do that. . . ."

These had been difficult statements to make for the man who believed that "those who deny freedom to others deserve it not for themselves, and under a just God can not long retain it." But now Lincoln grasped at Lee's retreat as the opportunity for doing what was in his heart. On December 1, 1862, in his annual message to Congress, he informed the nation of the historic step he was about to take. "That on the first day of January, . . . all persons held as slaves within any State or designated part of a State, the people whereof shall then be in rebellion against the United States, shall be then, thenceforward, and forever free."

Upon hearing Lincoln's words, the great African American leader Frederick Douglass exclaimed that the Civil War had suddenly been "invested with sanctity." He was right. Thanks to Abraham Lincoln, the war to save the Union had also become the war to free the slaves.

Ex-slave Frederick Douglass, center, became the leading black spokesman for African American rights. Blanche Kelso Bruce, left, and Hiram Revels, right, would become the first African Americans elected to the U.S. Senate, in 1875 and 1870 respectively.

Opposite: Following the Emancipation Proclamation, thousands of African American men were accepted into the Union army, where they made an enormous contribution. A member of Mathew B. Brady's photographic corps captured this image of African American soldiers posing with Union officers at their camp at Brandy Station, Virginia.

Gettysburg

Lincoln's proclamation to free the slaves had made the South more determined than ever to preserve its way of life. In June 1863, Lee was ready to attempt once again an invasion of the North. He led his troops across Maryland and into Pennsylvania, the farthest penetration that the Confederacy had made into Union territory.

Lincoln, meanwhile, had turned control of the Union armies over to General George Meade. And on July 1, 1863, Meade's Union army confronted Lee and his troops as they tried to continue their march through Pennsylvania.

The two vast armies, numbering more than 170,000 men, met on what became an enormous battlefield outside the small country town of Gettysburg. It would be a three-day engagement, to this day the largest battle ever fought on the North American continent. On the first day, the Union troops fought a delaying action. The next day Lee launched a vicious assault, attacking the full-strength Northern forces on both of their flanks. But the heavy Union artillery beat back each of the Confederate attacks. On the third day, Lee decided upon a desperate measure. He ordered 12,000 men, under the command of General George E. Pickett, to make an all-out charge across an open mile of the battlefield in the hope of wiping out the vital center of the Union forces. Pickett's men managed to penetrate the Union line, but only briefly. Overcome by the murderous Northern fire, the surviving 7,000 of Pickett's men were forced to turn back.

This bold gamble had resulted in a vital and decisive Confederate defeat. More than 50,000 brave combatants lay dead. As for Robert E. Lee, he had no choice but to retreat back into Virginia for a second time. Even though more fighting remained, never again would Confederate troops set foot on Northern soil.

Union soldiers overlooking a supply base.

Opposite: Although their cameras were still primitive, Civil War photographers were able to produce some masterful images. This photograph of captured Confederate soldiers at Gettysburg has been attributed to Alexander Gardner.

An Immortal Address

"That this nation, under God, shall have a new birth of freedom—and that government of the people, by the people, for the people, shall not perish from the earth."

The victory at Gettysburg had been won at a terrible human price. Some two months later, Lincoln received a letter informing him that the state of Pennsylvania had decided to purchase seventeen acres for a cemetery to honor those who had sacrificed their lives at Gettysburg. A committee had invited the nation's most celebrated orator, Edward Everett, to be the main speaker at the dedication ceremonies. Almost as an afterthought, the committee decided to invite Lincoln to participate in the ceremonies by delivering "a few appropriate remarks."

Lincoln had been told that as many as 20,000 people were certain to attend the dedication. What better opportunity of charging his fellow citizens with the mission of carrying out the cause for which so many had given their lives?

Yes, he decided, he must go, and on November 19, 1863, he sat patiently on the platform as Edward Everett delivered a two-hour, 13,607-word oration. Then it was Lincoln's turn. Many in the huge crowd had grown restless during Everett's long speech. Slowly Lincoln stood, took off his shawl, and put on his steel-rimmed spectacles. Then he removed his tall silk hat and took from it the speech he was about to deliver.

Four score and seven years ago our fathers brought forth on this continent, a new nation, conceived in Liberty, and dedicated to the proposition that all men are created equal.

Now we are engaged in a great civil war, testing whether that nation, or any nation so conceived and so dedicated, can long endure. We are met on a great battle-field of that war. We have come to dedicate a portion of that field, as a final resting place for those who here gave their lives that that nation might live. It is altogether fitting and proper that we should do this.

But, in a larger sense, we can not dedicate—we can not consecrate—we can not hallow—this ground. The brave men, living and dead, who struggled here, have consecrated it, far above our poor power to add or detract. The world will little note, nor long remember what we say here, but it can never forget what they did here. It is for us the living, rather, to be dedicated here to the unfinished work which they who fought here have thus far so nobly advanced. It is rather for us to be here dedicated to the great task remaining before us—that from these honored dead we take increased devotion to that cause for which they gave the last full measure of devotion—that we here highly resolve that these dead shall not have died in vain—that this nation, under God, shall have a new birth of freedom—and that government of the people, by the people, for the people, shall not perish from the earth.

Almost before many in the crowd were aware that it had begun, the speech was over. Ten sentences—less than 300 words—little more than two minutes long. There was only a smattering of applause, a few short hand claps. And as Lincoln sat down, he was sure that the speech was a failure.

But he was wrong. On the platform, when Secretary of State William Seward was asked if he had helped the president write the speech, Seward replied, "No one but Abraham Lincoln could have made that address."

Opposite: Recently, much publicity was given to a photograph long contained in the collections of the Library of Congress that shows a view of the crowd attending the Gettysburg Address. When enlarged (inset), far in the background a figure on horseback wearing a high hat similar to the type Lincoln wore is revealed. Is it Lincoln? For now, no one is certain.

Lincoln?

Lincoln and Thanksgiving

"I do therefore invite my fellow citizens in every part of the United States . . . to set apart and observe the last Thursday of November next, as a day of Thanksgiving and Praise to our beneficent Father who dwelleth in the Heavens."

Among Abraham Lincoln's many accomplishments is one for which he is not generally known. It was Lincoln who, only one week after delivering his Gettysburg Address, made Thanksgiving a national holiday to be celebrated on the same day in every state.

The national holiday we now know as Thanksgiving came about as the result of the tireless efforts of a remarkable woman named Sarah Josepha Hale, author of the poem "Mary Had a Little Lamb." She wanted to make Thanksgiving a national holiday. And she believed that in Abraham Lincoln, she had just the person to make that happen.

She was right. Through editorials she wrote and an impassioned letter she sent to the president, Hale convinced Lincoln that the time was appropriate for the establishment of such a holiday. Actually, Lincoln needed little convincing. By the time Hale made her plea, the tide of the Civil War finally seemed to be turning in the Union's favor. For the first time, Lincoln began to believe that the Union would survive. There was indeed much to be thankful for.

On October 3, 1863, the president issued his Thanksgiving Proclamation, explaining as only Lincoln could, why, despite the horror and tragedy of civil war, it was appropriate to give thanks. "The year that is drawing towards its close, has been filled with the blessings of fruitful fields and healthful skies. In the midst of a civil war of unequaled magnitude and severity . . . peace has been preserved with all nations, order has been maintained, the laws have been respected and obeyed, and harmony has prevailed everywhere except in the theatre of military conflict. . . . No human counsel hath devised nor hath any mortal hand worked out these great things. They are the gracious gifts of the Most High God, who, while dealing with us in anger for our sins, hath nevertheless remembered mercy."

Contrary to popular belief, Thanksgiving did not begin with the Pilgrims. Their celebration was a harvest festival, an event that had taken place for hundreds of years in many nations throughout the world.

Opposite: This photograph of Abraham Lincoln, taken at the time he issued his Thanksgiving Proclamation, shows a president who, for the first time since the start of the Civil War, was beginning to feel confident that the tide of the war had turned in the Union's favor.

Lincoln Finds a General

"He doesn't worry and bother me. He isn't shrieking for reinforcements all the time. He takes what troops we can safely give him . . . and does the best he can with what he has got."

The victory at Gettysburg and the success of his speech at that battlefield had done much to lift Lincoln's spirits. And he had another reason for optimism. He had, at last, found a military commander who, he believed, could bring the war to a successful conclusion. It was Ulysses S. Grant who, only three days after the Battle of Gettysburg, had forced the largest Confederate fortification remaining on the Mississippi to surrender. Not everyone in Lincoln's administration was enamored of Grant. When, after the Battle of Shiloh, they had complained that Grant was too brutal an officer, Lincoln had replied, "I can't spare this man. He fights." When his advisors and others criticized Grant for drinking too heavily, he told them he wished he knew the brand of liquor that Grant was fond of drinking so he could send some to all the other Northern generals. On March 9, Lincoln appointed Grant commander of all the Union armies.

Within weeks, Grant and Lincoln devised a plan that they hoped would bring an end to the Confederacy and the war. Grant, with an army of some 100,000 men, would march toward the Confederate capital at Richmond, Virginia, to engage Robert E. Lee's main army and hopefully gain the total victory that had not been accomplished at either Antietam or Gettysburg. Meanwhile, Grant's subordinate, General William Tecumseh Sherman, also with 100,000 troops, would march toward the city of Atlanta in the hope of capturing both that Confederate city and, even more important, its vital railroad yards.

Aside from Ulysses S. Grant, William Tecumseh Sherman was the most noteworthy of the Union generals. Celebrated as a brilliant military strategist, he was also criticized for the harshness of the way in which he destroyed Southern cities in the campaigns that brought an end to the Civil War.

Opposite: According to Matthew B. Brady, this is the last photograph taken of Grant in the field, taken just before the battles of Spotsylvania and Cold Harbor.

Events Sway an Election

"I have not permitted myself, gentlemen, to conclude that I am the best man in the country; but I am reminded, in this connection, of a story of an old Dutch farmer, who remarked to a companion once that 'it was not best to swap horses when crossing streams.'"

Given the plan that he and General Grant had put into motion, Lincoln knew that it was a most critical time in the war. But despite that, and everything else he had to attend to, it was now time to run for reelection. And even though he had given his heart, his soul, and even much of his health to saving the Union, his reelection was far from a certainty.

But just two months before voters went to the polls, startling news arrived. General Sherman had captured Atlanta and had destroyed its railroad yards, army facilities, factories, and warehouses. The Confederacy had lost its most valuable remaining center of transportation and supplies.

The news was more than enough to sway the election. In fact, Lincoln won by a landslide. Commenting on his reelection he told supporters, "I earnestly believe that [my reelection] will be to the lasting advantage, if not the very salvation of the country."

The speech that Lincoln delivered on March 4, 1865, was much shorter than his first inaugural address, in which he had valiantly attempted to avoid a civil war. Now, with the end of the tragic conflict at last in sight, he had an equally well-defined purpose. His speech was a plea both for reconciliation and for a renewal of resolve. It was an emotional address, urging the North to be magnanimous toward the soon-to-be-defeated South and to dedicate itself to putting the nation back together. It ended with what many historians regard as Lincoln's finest statement, greater even than the immortal lines in his Gettysburg Address. "With malice toward none," Lincoln stated, "with charity for all; with firmness in right, as God gives us to see the right, let us strive to finish the work we are in; to bind up the nation's wounds; to care for him who shall have borne the battle, and for his widow, and his orphan—to do all which may achieve and cherish a just, and a lasting peace, among ourselves, and with all nations."

An anti-Lincoln cartoon showing opposition to Lincoln's reelection. In the cartoon, a woman symbolizing the United States asks the president to give back the half million men who, at that point, had been killed in the Civil War.

Opposite: Members of William T. Sherman's troops tear up the railroad tracks in Atlanta. By destroying the South's main transportation facilities, Sherman put an end to any chances of a Confederate victory.

"The ballot is stronger than the bullet."

It was through the camera that the most remarkable events in Abraham Lincoln's life were revealed, events that not only disclosed but shaped his life as well. No single Lincoln photograph is more extraordinary than the one on the opposite page. On the surface, it is a picture taken during Lincoln's Second Inaugural Address, a picture not unlike the inaugural photographs of most U.S. presidents. But a closer examination of the photograph reveals something that can only be regarded as astounding.

According to renowned Lincoln historians Dorothy Meserve Kunhardt and Philip B. Kunhardt, Jr., the figure in the high stovepipe hat standing on the railed platform in the upper right of the photograph and looking directly down on the president is John Wilkes Booth, the man who, only forty-one days later, would fire the bullet that would end Abraham Lincoln's life. Booth attended the inaugural as the guest of his fiancée, Lucy Hale, whose father was a U.S. Senator from New Hampshire. Later Booth would state, "What an excellent chance I had to kill the president, if I had wished, on inauguration day."

Just as startling, standing directly beneath Lincoln's podium are, according to the Kunhardts, five of the men who would be key figures in Lincoln's assassination.

Left to right: George Atzerodt—he was supposed to kill newly elected Vice President Andrew Johnson but lost his nerve; Lewis Powell (aka Lewis Paine)—attacked Seward's son and bodyguard before stabbing Seward; Edman Spangler—he worked at Ford's Theatre as a carpenter and scene shifter and helped Booth escape after the assassination; John Surratt—though part of the conspiracy, Surratt was in Elmira, New York, on a spying mission on the day of the assassination; David Herold—he accompanied Powell to Seward's house and stood watch.

Opposite: Lincoln is missing from the podium in this photograph because the photographer's stray fingerprint wiped him off the negative, but amazingly, the conspirators in his assassination are visible.

Booth

Herold

Powell

Surratt

Atzerodt

Spangler

Sherman's March

Shortly after delivering his Second Inaugural Address, Lincoln was handed the best news he had received since the Civil War began. The plan that he and Grant had devised was working even beyond his fondest expectations. After taking control of Atlanta, General Sherman had marched his army northward all the way to the sea, capturing Charlestown, South Carolina, in the process. Sherman's forces were now headed toward Richmond, where Grant was already establishing a stranglehold on Lee's army.

Within a month, the news got even better. On April 2, 1865, Lee informed Confederate president Jefferson Davis that he could no longer protect Richmond and that Davis and the rest of his government would have to flee the city. One day later, Union troops took control of the Confederate capital. On April 9, 1865, almost exactly four years to the day that the bloodshed began, Robert E. Lee met with Ulysses S. Grant at the Appomattox Courthouse in Virginia and surrendered the Confederate army. The Civil War was over.

The terms of the surrender were generous. All Confederate soldiers who owned the horses that they had brought with them to the war would be allowed to keep them. And, as Grant stated, "Each officer and man will be allowed to return to his home not to be disturbed by the United States authorities. . . ."

As soon as the signing was completed, a sad and weary Robert E. Lee left the courthouse, mounted his horse, and rode slowly away. Immediately, Union artillerymen began firing their cannons in celebration. But Grant, respectful of what had been a gallant foe, ordered them to halt. "We did not want," Grant would later write in his memoirs, "to exult over their downfall."

There were no cameras allowed inside the room where Lee surrendered to Grant. What was taken, however, was this photograph showing Union soldiers outside the Appomattox Courthouse in which the surrender took place.

Opposite: Ruins of Richmond, Virginia. General William T. Sherman's devastating march through the South resulted in the almost total destruction of the Confederate capital.

The Price of a Presidency

"To His care commending you, as I hope in your prayers you will commend me, I bid you an affectionate farewell."

No president of the United States has ever carried as great a burden as did Abraham Lincoln. It was a burden that took both an enormous physical and mental toll on the man called upon to save a nation, one that in only five years changed his appearance dramatically.

"The face of Lincoln told the story of his life," wrote journalist Allen Thorndike Rice, "a life of sorrow and struggle, of ceaseless endeavor. [Lincoln's] rugged energy was stamped on that . . . face, with its great brows and bones and the deep melancholy that overshadowed every feature of it."

Mary Livermore, a family friend who visited the Lincolns regularly, stated, "No one can estimate the suffering endured by President Lincoln during the war. Each time [I saw him] I was impressed with the look of pain and weariness stereotyped on his face. He envied the soldier sleeping in his blanket on the Potomac, he would say in his torture. And, sometimes when the woes of the country pressed most heavily on him, he envied the dead soldier sleeping in the cemetery."

As telling as these words were, nothing could more dramatically reveal the terrible price Lincoln paid than by comparing what he looked like in this 1860 photograph, when he campaigned for the presidency, and the photo long regarded as the last one ever taken of him alive, shown opposite, just five years later.

A Frightening Premonition

"Although it was only a dream, I have been strangely annoyed by it ever since."

In early April 1865, Lincoln recounted a haunting dream to his wife and colleagues. "I could not have been long in bed when I fell into a slumber, for I was weary. I soon began to dream. There seemed to be a death-like stillness about me. . . . Determined to find the cause of a state of things so mysterious and so shocking, I kept on until I arrived at the East Room, which I entered. . . . Before me was a catafalque, on which rested a corpse wrapped in funeral vestments. Around it were stationed soldiers who were acting as guards; . . . 'Who is dead in the White House?' I demanded of one of the soldiers. 'The President,' was his answer; 'he was killed by an assassin!' Then came a loud burst of grief from the crowd, which awoke me from my dream."

On the morning of April 14, 1865, however, Abraham Lincoln was not thinking of death. Five days earlier the horrific war had ended. Part of his good humor was also due to the fact that that evening, he and his wife were going to Ford's Theatre to see the play *Our American Cousin*.

Abraham Lincoln would be assassinated that night by John Wilkes Booth, one of the country's most promising actors. A white supremacist who believed that "slavery was one of the greatest blessings that God ever bestowed on a favored nation," Booth had been hatching a plot with fellow conspirators. His original plan was to kidnap Lincoln and ransom him in exchange for an immediate end to the war, with the Union's coming to terms favorable to the South. By the second week of April, however, Booth had decided that kidnapping was too mild a punishment for the man who had freed the slaves. Lincoln must die.

SATAN TEMPTING BOOTH TO THE MURDER OF THE PRESIDENT.

Not surprisingly, John Wilkes Booth's assassination of Abraham Lincoln was the most reported event of its day. In this drawing, Booth's murder of the president is attributed to his having been influenced by the devil.

Opposite: When this photograph was taken shortly before John Wilkes Booth murdered Abraham Lincoln, Booth was regarded as an accomplished actor. No one at the time could have suspected that he would soon commit one of history's most infamous crimes.

Even crazed with anger, Booth planned Lincoln's assassination carefully and ingeniously. While picking up his mail at Ford's Theatre on the morning of April 14, Booth learned that Lincoln would be attending the play that night.

Immediately, Booth put into action a plan that he had been developing ever since he had decided to kill, rather than kidnap, the president. That afternoon he snuck back into the theater and secretly climbed up to the presidential box. Reaching the door leading to the box, he drilled a hole in it to give him a clear view of the back of the rocking chair in which he knew Lincoln would be sitting. Now, when it came time to murder the president, he would have a clear sight of his target before entering the box.

At nine thirty that evening, Booth returned to Ford's Theatre on horseback, leaving his horse with a young accomplice to be used as a means of escape once the assassination was carried out. He climbed the stairs to the presidential box and peered in through the hole he had made in the door. Booth could clearly see the back of Lincoln's head.

Shortly before ten thirty, with the play about halfway over, John Wilkes Booth turned the doorknob, stepped inside, placed a small derringer-type pistol next to the back of Abraham Lincoln's head, and fired. Dense smoke surrounded the president's head as his wife struggled desperately to keep him from pitching forward over the railing of the box.

As Mary Todd Lincoln began shouting for help, the audience came alive. "Stop that man," someone screamed. Shouts of "Hang him! Hang him!" rang out through the theater. Then someone cried out the word "Booth." Soon almost the entire audience took up the cry and shouts of "Booth! Booth!" filled the air. Playgoer Helen Truman would later recall, "Cries of terror created a pandemonium that . . . through all the ages will stand out in my memory as the hell of hells."

This drawing of Booth shooting Lincoln shows those who were sitting in the presidential box when the president was killed—Major Henry Rathbone; his fiancée, Clara Harris; and Mary Todd Lincoln.

Opposite: These two photographs show Ford's Theatre at the time Lincoln was assassinated—the exterior of the building on top, and the presidential box where Lincoln's murder took place below.

Twenty-three-year-old Dr. Charles Leale made his way to the presidential box to try to save America's leader. Laying the unconscious Lincoln on the floor, he saw that the president was not breathing and that blood was oozing from a perfectly smooth bullet hole in his head. At this point, another twenty-three-year-old doctor, Charles Taft, half climbed and was half pushed into the presidential box. While Taft began pumping Lincoln's arms, trying to restore circulation, Leale frantically massaged the president's chest above his heart. Suddenly the heart fluttered and Lincoln began to breathe again. But Leale knew that it was only temporary. Looking around him at those in the now-crowded box, he sadly proclaimed, "It is impossible for him to recover."

By this time, Laura Keene, the star of the play, had been admitted to the presidential box. Receiving permission from the two doctors, she placed Lincoln's head in her lap and dabbed his forehead with water as the president's

blood spread across her elegant yellow satin skirt. Someone had sent for the presidential carriage to bring the stricken Lincoln back to the White House, but Leale and Taft were convinced that the bumpy carriage ride would diminish whatever slim chances the president had of surviving.

Instead, as soldiers cleared a path through the large crowd that had already gathered outside the theater, the sixteenth president of the United States was carried across the street to a boardinghouse and placed upon a bed in one of the boarder's rooms. For the next nine hours, Lincoln would be treated by no less than sixteen doctors. But Leale had been right. There was no hope. At 7:22 a.m., Abraham Lincoln became the last great casualty of the Civil War.

Soldiers line a main boulevard in New York prior to that city's funeral procession.

Opposite: Photographers were not allowed in the room where Abraham Lincoln lay mortally wounded. None of the scores of artists' depictions of the scene were completely accurate. Collectively, however, they showed almost all of the people who, at one time or another, were at the president's deathbed.

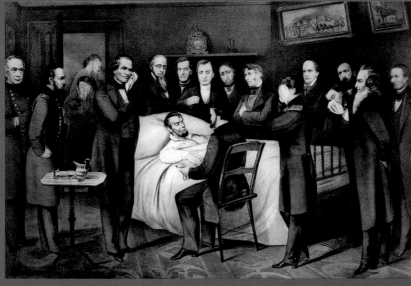

When Abraham Lincoln was shot at Ford's Theatre on April 14, 1865, he was carrying two pairs of eyeglasses, a lens polisher, a pocketknife, a watch fob, a linen handkerchief, and a brown leather wallet. There is certainly nothing unusual about these common items. But other articles taken from the assassinated president's pockets have puzzled Lincoln scholars.

Inside Lincoln's wallet was a five-dollar Confederate note. No one can say for sure why he had such an item in his possession, but some have speculated he carried it as a reminder of the rebel government that had been finally defeated just three days earlier with the surrender of Confederate general Robert E. Lee to Union commander Ulysses S. Grant at Appomattox, Virginia. Also in Lincoln's pockets were nine newspaper clippings, some favorable to the president and his policies.

Today all these items are housed at the Library of Congress in Washington. They were first put on display in 1976 by Librarian of Congress Daniel Boorstin, who believed that their exposure to the public would help humanize a man who had become, as Boorstin stated, "mythologically engulfed."

Since that time, the contents of Lincoln's pockets have become among the items that visitors to the Library most often ask to see.

This is the derringer with which John Wilkes Booth shot Abraham Lincoln. Today it is housed in the museum in Ford's Theatre.

Opposite: The contents of Abraham Lincoln's pockets on the night he was assassinated remain a vivid reminder of one of history's most tragic acts. These items are often displayed with this copy of the *New York Times* announcing Lincoln's assassination.

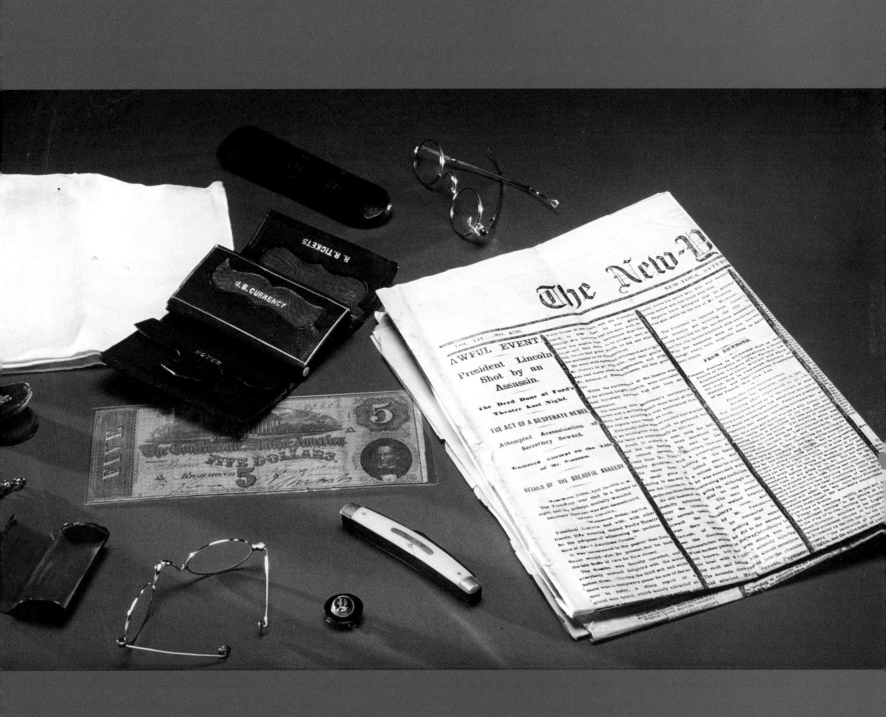

The Long Road Home

Abraham Lincoln's assassination initiated the most intense period of mourning the nation had ever experienced. Lincoln, the first American president to be assassinated, was given several funerals, each the largest ever held to that date in the United States. When the casket carrying his body was taken by horse-drawn wagon from the White House to the Capitol to lie in state, 40,000 mourners, most of them weeping, looked on in silent tribute. The next morning, the first individuals permitted to enter were thousands of wounded Civil War soldiers, anxious to pay their respects to their fallen commander in chief. Then the public at large was let in—3,000 per hour—more than 25,000 on the first day alone.

When the Capitol viewing was completed, the coffin was placed on a seven-car train containing a special burial car. It then embarked on a 1,200-mile journey, traveling the same route Lincoln had taken on his trip to his first inauguration. This time, even in the poorest districts, there were the symbols of mourning—black crepe, black ribbons, black drapery. And there were the crowds, tens of thousands of people at every stop and all along the train's route, standing silent and bareheaded, saying good-bye. He was at last laid to rest in his beloved Springfield's Oak Ridge Cemetery.

Lincoln was originally buried in a marble sarcophagus. In the years following his burial, however, attempts were made to steal his body, including a plot by a gang of counterfeiters to hold the body for ransom. The evildoers actually succeeded in entering Lincoln's tomb before they were apprehended.

In 1900, Robert Lincoln, concerned about future threats, instructed that a much larger and far more secure tomb be built. In September 1901, Lincoln's body was placed in a magnificent new crypt. To prevent any further attempts on the body, the coffin was encased in concrete several feet thick, surrounded by a cage, and buried beneath a rock slab. Abraham Lincoln could finally rest in peace.

This photograph shows workers removing Lincoln's casket from one resting place in Oak Ridge Cemetery before transferring it to another spot in the burial grounds in order to prevent criminals from stealing it and holding it for ransom.

Opposite: Abraham Lincoln's final resting place provides a fitting tribute to the man who, through his determination and genius, saved his nation.

The Secret Photograph

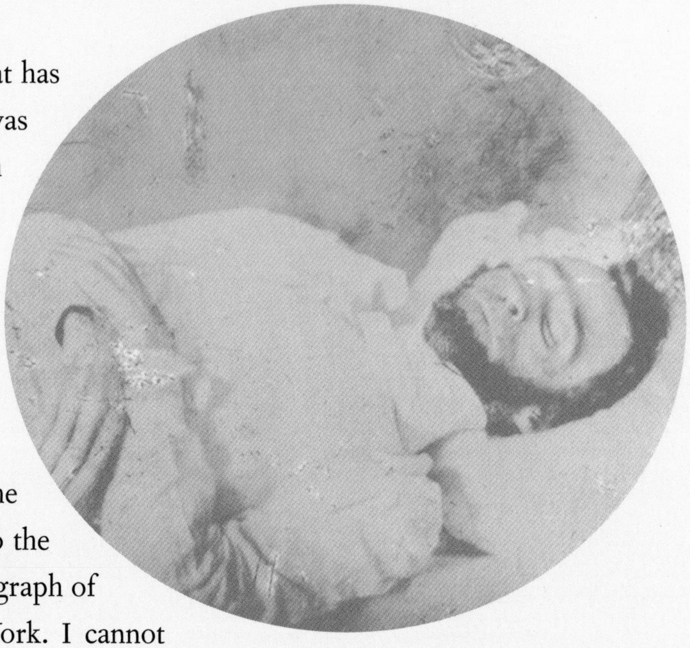

The only photograph of Abraham Lincoln in death that has been preserved, shown opposite, has a remarkable history. It was one of a number of photographs that photographer Jeremiah Gurney, Jr., took of the assassinated president lying in state in New York City Hall before thousands of people were let in to view Lincoln's body. Knowing that photographs of the dead president would be regarded as in extremely bad taste—and even disgraceful—Gurney took his pictures in secret from a gallery high above where the body lay guarded by federal officers.

When Secretary of War Edwin Stanton became aware that the photographs had been taken, he immediately sent a telegram to the officer in charge. It read: "I see by the newspapers that a photograph of the corpse . . . was allowed to be taken yesterday in New York. I cannot sufficiently express my surprise and disapproval of such an act while the body was in your charge. . . . You will direct the provost-marshall to go to the photographer, seize and destroy the plates and any pictures or engravings that may have been made, and consider yourself responsible if the offense is repeated."

This was done, except for the fact that one small print survived. In 1953, a fifteen-year-old boy found the picture hidden away in the Illinois State Historical Library. It remains one of the most notable of all the thousands of Lincoln photographs.

Following Abraham Lincoln's death, a number of photographs purporting to be of Lincoln lying in his coffin appeared. All, like this one, were proven to be fakes.

Opposite: New York City Hall was one of several places where Abraham Lincoln's body lay in state. The New York public viewing was the last in which the president's coffin was kept open.

Almost at the exact same time that John Wilkes Booth had fired his fatal shot at Abraham Lincoln, one of his accomplices, a huge, brutish man named Lewis Powell, was carrying out another part of Booth's evil plot by entering William H. Seward's home and slashing Lincoln's secretary of state across the neck with a knife. Although seriously wounded, Seward survived the attack.

Immediately after the two assaults, an enormous manhunt for Booth, Powell, and the other conspirators was launched. Scores of different types of posters, announcing huge rewards for the capture of Booth and his accomplices, were printed and widely distributed. The poster on the facing page was different from the others. It was the first reward poster ever created using photographs rather than drawings to identify the persons being sought.

The images used to provide exact likenesses of the hunted men were a special type of photograph. They were called *cartes-des-visite,* and throughout the last decade of Abraham Lincoln's life they were extremely popular. Introduced in 1854 by Frenchman Adolphe Eugene Disderi, *carte-de-visite* in French means "visiting card," and that is how millions of them were used. Produced in a camera that enabled as many as twelve of the same *cartes* to be produced on a single negative, the photographs were very inexpensive. It became common practice to leave a *carte* behind after making a social or business call. People also exchanged the photographic cards during holidays and birthday celebrations. *Cartes-des-visite* were also used by store owners who pasted images of their products in bound catalogs to show customers the range of their goods beyond those they could display in their store. By the time Abraham Lincoln first ran for president in 1860, *cartes-des-visite* had become particularly popular with politicians, who distributed them by the thousands during their campaigns for office.

This *carte-de-visite* was distributed to Lincoln supporters throughout his campaign for reelection.

Opposite: The rewards offered for the capture of John Wilkes Booth and his fellow conspirators, who were still at large when this poster was printed, were, by far, the largest ever offered.

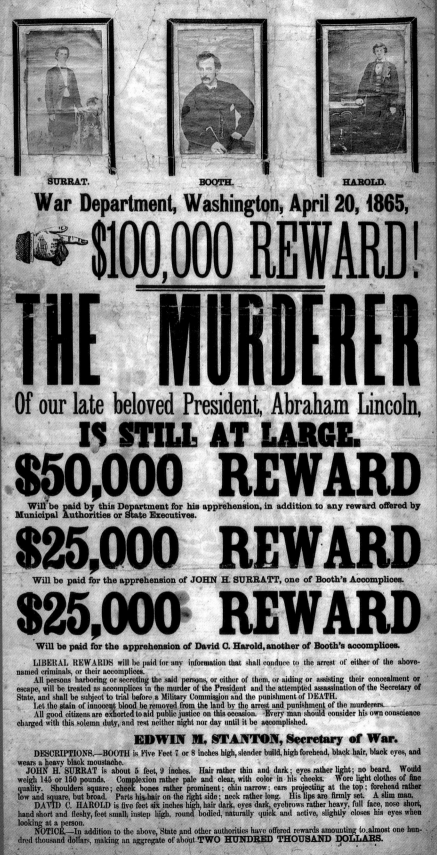

SURRAT.   BOOTH.   HAROLD.

War Department, Washington, April 20, 1865,

$100,000 REWARD!

THE MURDERER

Of our late beloved President, Abraham Lincoln,

IS STILL AT LARGE.

$50,000 REWARD

Will be paid by this Department for his apprehension, in addition to any reward offered by Municipal Authorities or State Executives.

$25,000 REWARD

Will be paid for the apprehension of JOHN H. SURRATT, one of Booth's Accomplices.

$25,000 REWARD

Will be paid for the apprehension of David C. Harold, another of Booth's accomplices.

LIBERAL REWARDS will be paid for any information that shall conduce to the arrest of either of the above-named criminals, or their accomplices.

All persons harboring or secreting the said persons, or either of them, or aiding or assisting their concealment or escape, will be treated as accomplices in the murder of the President and the attempted assassination of the Secretary of State, and shall be subject to trial before a Military Commission and the punishment of DEATH.

Let the stain of innocent blood be removed from the land by the arrest and punishment of the murderers.

All good citizens are exhorted to aid public justice on this occasion. Every man should consider his own conscience charged with this solemn duty, and rest neither night nor day until it be accomplished.

EDWIN M. STANTON, Secretary of War.

DESCRIPTIONS.—BOOTH is Five Feet 7 or 8 inches high, slender build, high forehead, black hair, black eyes, and wears a heavy black moustache.

JOHN H. SURRAT is about 5 feet, 9 inches. Hair rather thin and dark; eyes rather light; no beard. Would weigh 145 or 150 pounds. Complexion rather pale and clear, with color in his cheeks. Wore light clothes of fine quality. Shoulders square; cheek bones rather prominent; chin narrow; ears projecting at the top; forehead rather low and square, but broad. Parts his hair on the right side; neck rather long. His lips are firmly set. A slim man.

DAVID C. HAROLD is five feet six inches high, hair dark, eyes dark, eyebrows rather heavy, full face, nose short, hand short and fleshy, feet small, instep high, round bodied, naturally quick and active, slightly closes his eyes when looking at a person.

NOTICE.—In addition to the above, State and other authorities have offered rewards amounting to almost one hundred thousand dollars, making an aggregate of about **TWO HUNDRED THOUSAND DOLLARS.**

After shooting Abraham Lincoln, John Wilkes Booth leaped from the presidential box, breaking his leg on the floor below. Once he fled Ford's Theatre, he made his way on horseback to the home of Dr. Samuel Mudd, who treated the fractured limb. Joined by coconspirator David Herold, Booth then made his way through southern Maryland and across the Potomac and Rappahannock rivers into Virginia. Meanwhile, Union soldiers, led by Lieutenant Edward Doherty and accompanied by two Secret Service men, had picked up his trail. Early on the morning of April 26, 1865, they found him hiding with Herold in a barn near Bowling Green, Virginia.

As soon as the soldiers surrounded the barn, Doherty ordered Booth and Herold to give themselves up. Herold immediately complied, but Booth refused to budge. Doherty then ordered that the barn be set afire in order to drive the murderer out. Even with the building totally engulfed in flames, Booth still did not come out. At this point, one of the soldiers, a religious fanatic named Boston Corbett, believing he had heard a voice from heaven ordering him to avenge Lincoln's death, suddenly fired a shot into the barn that struck Booth in the neck. Despite the roaring flames, a group of soldiers pulled the mortally wounded Booth from the barn and carried him to a nearby porch, where he died two and a half hours later.

As the result of an enormous dragnet ordered by Secretary of War Edwin Stanton, all of the suspects were quickly captured, tried, and found guilty. They included Dr. Mudd, who, at the time, may or may not have known it was Lincoln's assassin whose leg he was treating. Also sentenced to death was Mary Surratt, the mother of one of the conspirators, in whose home meetings between the plotters had taken place. To this day it is not known how much of the assassins' plans she actually knew.

This photograph of John Wilkes Booth was taken in a morgue eleven days after he was shot to death.

Opposite: Left to right, the bodies of Mary Surratt, Lewis Powell, David Herold, and George Atzerodt hang from the gallows.

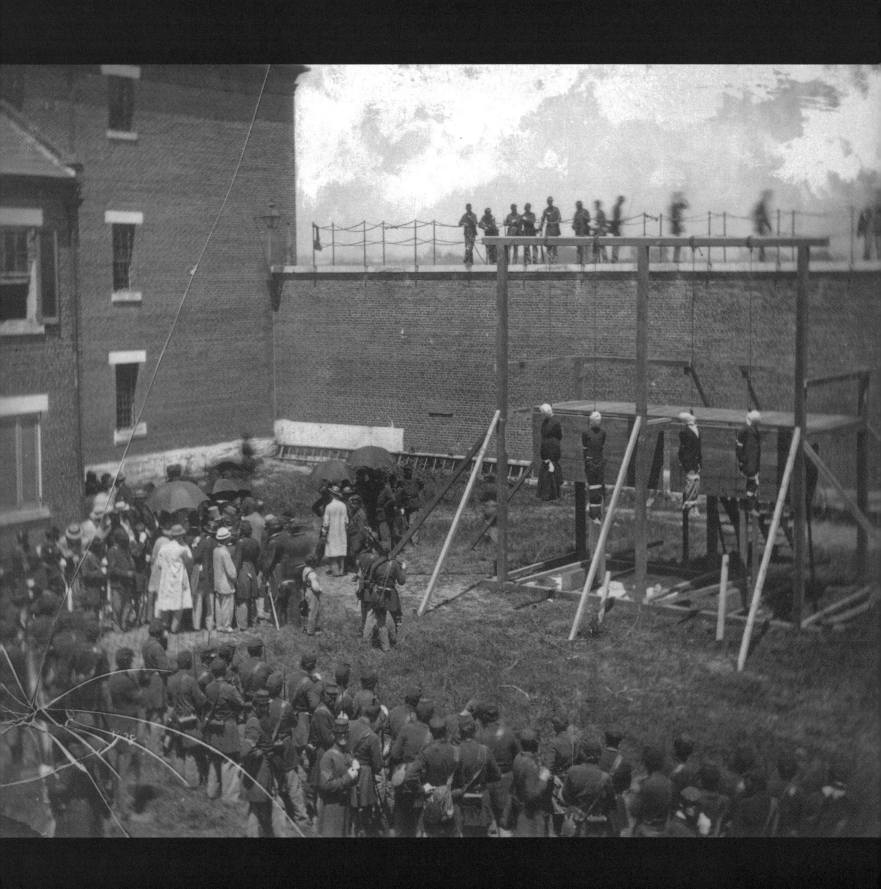

From the moment he became president, practically every waking hour of Abraham Lincoln's life was occupied with waging the Civil War. Yet, during his time in the White House, he also managed to oversee other affairs that would result in enormous benefits to the nation. Among them was his authorization of the construction of the nation's first transcontinental railroad. It was an act that he signed on May 20, 1862, however, that had the most far-reaching non–Civil War related effects of all.

At the time, most of the land in the United States west of the Mississippi, amounting to millions of acres, remained unsettled. The Homestead Act, which Lincoln championed, offered 160 acres of land free to anyone who—after paying an eighteen-dollar filing fee—claimed, occupied, and made improvements on the property for at least five years. It was an act that changed the nation. Among the hundreds of thousands of people who crossed the Mississippi to stake their claims were legions of factory workers from the East who were unhappy with

the drudgery and low wages their labor brought them. They were joined by millions of oppressed immigrants from Europe anxious to accept the offer of free land in a free country.

By 1900, thanks to the Homestead Act, more than eighty million acres in the West had been settled and more than 372,000 farms had been created. Those who built the farms would face enormous challenges—droughts, prairie fires, mass invasions of insects in summer, devastating blizzards in winter. But they would turn the once untamed prairie into a breadbasket, feeding not only America but much of the world as well.

Abraham Lincoln's authorization of the building of the transcontinental railroad changed the nation. When it was completed on May 10, 1869, the United States was united by rail.

Opposite: Life was not easy for the men, women, and children we have come to know as the pioneers. But the Homestead Act gave them the opportunity to build better lives than they had previously known.

Abraham Lincoln's journey was over. But, like so many of the words he spoke, he would become immortal. Every passing year would bring the increased realization that a giant had walked on the national stage.

His words inspired first a nation and then the world. But so, too, did the character and life of a man born in the backwoods of Kentucky, who rose to such heights with less than a year of formal education. Perhaps the most telling assessments of all came from two key figures on opposite sides of the conflict that was the pivotal event in Lincoln's life. Hearing of Lincoln's assassination, Robert E. Lee informed those around him that he had surrendered the Confederate Army as much to his faith in Abraham Lincoln's honesty and compassion as to Ulysses S. Grant's artillery. William T. Sherman, the Union general whose conquest of Atlanta put an end to Lee's hopes in the struggle, put it this way: "Of all the men I ever met," he declared, "[Abraham Lincoln possessed] more of the elements of greatness combined with goodness, than any other."

At the Lincoln Memorial, Lincoln's hands appear to form the symbols for the letters A and L—his initials—in American Sign Language. But scholars are not sure if the sculptor, Daniel Chester French, intended the subtle message or if the pose is a coincidence.

Places to Visit

The following sites provide living reminders of Abraham Lincoln's life and career and the times in which he lived. All have special exhibits and programs of special interest to young people and are fun to visit:

Abraham Lincoln Birthplace National Historic Site Sinking Spring Farm

2995 Lincoln Farm Road
Hodgenville, Kentucky 42748
For information: 270-358-3137
www.nps.gov/abli/

This site's large marble building contains an exact replica of the Kentucky log cabin in which Abraham Lincoln was born. Other attractions include the Lincoln family Bible and a film about Lincoln's early life in Kentucky.

Ford's Theatre National Historic Site

511 10th Street, NW
Washington DC 20004
For information: 202-426-6924
www.fordstheatre.org

At this site, one can view the presidential box in which Abraham Lincoln was assassinated by John Wilkes Booth. The museum, housed on the building's bottom floor, contains artifacts connected with the assassination, including the derringer with which Booth murdered Lincoln and the hunting knife that he brandished during the attack.

Gettysburg National Military Park

97 Taneytown Road
Gettysburg, Pennsylvania 17325
For information: 717-334-1124 ext. 431
www.nps.gov/gett

This site features tours of the Gettysburg battlefield, the cemetery where 6,000 of those killed in the battle are buried, and the site of Abraham Lincoln's Gettysburg Address. The site's museum and visitors' center feature films on the battle and the address and contain a large collection of Civil War and Gettysburg artifacts.

The Lincoln Depot

10th and Monroe Streets
Springfield, Illinois 62703
For information: 217-544-8695
http://showcase.netins.net/web/creative/lincoln/sites/depot.htm

This is the place from which Lincoln left by train for the nation's capital, to be sworn in as the sixteenth president of the United States. It was from this depot that Lincoln delivered his farewell speech to his fellow Springfield citizens. The site features a video describing Lincoln's twelve-day journey to Washington DC.

Lincoln Log Cabin Site

400 South Lincoln Highway Road
Lerna, Illinois 62440
For information: 217-345-1845
www.lincolnlogcabin.org

This site preserves the last home and farm of Abraham Lincoln's father and stepmother. Along with an exact replica of Thomas Lincoln's Illinois home, the site features two "living history farms," where visitors may observe and experience 1840s Illinois farm life.

Lincoln Tomb State Historic Site

Oak Ridge Cemetery
Springfield, Illinois 62702
For information: 217-782-2717
http://showcase.netins.net/web/creative/lincoln/sites/tomb.htm

This is the site of the 117-foot-tall granite tomb in which Abraham Lincoln; Mary Todd Lincoln; and their sons Edward, William, and Tad are buried. (Robert Lincoln is buried in Arlington National Cemetery.) The magnificent memorial building contains several bronze statues accompanied by excerpts from Lincoln's speeches.

New Salem State Historic Site

15588 History Lane
Petersburg, Illinois 62675
For information: 217-632-4000
www.lincolnsnewsalem.com

This site features a re-creation of New Salem village, where Abraham Lincoln engaged in several occupations—including store clerk, laborer, surveyor, and postmaster—before becoming a lawyer and political leader. The site's visitors' center offers a film of the six years Lincoln spent in New Salem and features his surveying instruments and other artifacts of the period.

Further Reading and Surfing

Books

Armstrong, Jennifer. *Photo by Brady: A Picture of the Civil War.* New York: Atheneum, 2005.

Armstrong, Jennifer. *A Three-Minute Speech: Lincoln's Remarks at Gettysburg.* New York: Aladdin, 2003.

Bial, Raymond. *Where Lincoln Walked.* New York: Walker Books for Young Readers, 1998.

Davis, Kenneth C. *Don't Know Much About Abraham Lincoln.* New York: HarperTrophy, 2004.

Freedman, Russell. *Lincoln: A Photobiography.* New York: Clarion Books, 1987.

Giblin, James Cross. *Good Brother, Bad Brother: The Story of Edwin Booth & John Wilkes Booth.* New York: Clarion Books, 2005.

Holzer, Harold. *The President Is Shot! The Assassination of Abraham Lincoln.* Honesdale, PA: Boyds Mills Press, 2004.

Marrin, Albert. *Commander in Chief: Abraham Lincoln and the Civil War.* New York: Dutton, 2003.

McKissack, Patricia C., and Fredrick L. McKissack. *Days of Jubilee: The End of Slavery in the United States.* New York: Scholastic, 2003.

Web Sites

www.abrahamlincoln200.org

www.historyplace.com/lincoln

www.lmunet.edu/museum/index.html

http://showcase.netins.net/web/creative/lincoln.html

Sources

THE FOLLOWING SOURCES HAVE BEEN PARTICULARLY IMPORTANT IN PRESENTING KEY CONCEPTS IN THIS BOOK:

David Hackett Fischer's *Liberty and Freedom: A Visual History of America's Founding Ideas.* In this book, acclaimed historian Fischer convincingly describes and documents how Abraham Lincoln was among the first to use photography "in a systematic way for political purposes" and how "he took a very active part in the photographic construction of his own image."

Harold Holzer's *Lincoln at Cooper Union.* This book is invaluable in providing an understanding of why Lincoln's Cooper Union Speech, long overshadowed by other of his addresses, is of lasting importance and why Lincoln declared that it was this speech that made him president.

Dorothy Meserve Kunhardt and Philip B. Kunhardt, Jr.'s *Twenty Days.* This book, first published in 1965, remains one of the most vivid accounts of Abraham Lincoln's assassination and its aftermath. The book is particularly important for the way it documents the presence of John Wilkes Booth and fellow conspirators at Lincoln's Second Inaugural Address.

HERE IS A BIBLIOGRAPHY OF THE MOST SIGNIFICANT SOURCES I USED IN MY RESEARCH:

Catton, Bruce. *The American Heritage Picture History of the Civil War.* New York: American Heritage/Bonanza Books, 1982.

Donald, David Herbert. *Lincoln.* New York: Touchstone, 1996.

Fischer, David Hackett. *Liberty and Freedom: A Visual History of America's Founding Ideas.* New York: Oxford University Press, 2005.

Foner, Eric, and Olivia Mahoney. *A House Divided: America in the Age of Lincoln.* New York: Norton, 1990.

Holzer, Harold. *Lincoln at Cooper Union: The Speech That Made Abraham Lincoln President.* New York: Simon & Schuster, 2004.

Humes, James C. *The Wit & Wisdom of Abraham Lincoln: A Treasury of More Than 1,000 Quotations and Anecdotes.* New York: HarperCollins, 1996.

Kunhardt, Dorothy Meserve, and Philip B. Kunhardt, Jr. *Twenty Days.* New York: Harper & Row, 1965.

Kunhardt, Philip B., Jr., Philip B. Kunhardt, III, and Peter W. Kunhardt. *Lincoln: An Illustrated Biography.* New York: Knopf, 1992.

Lincoln, Abraham. *Selected Speeches and Writings.* New York: Vintage Books, 1992.

Sandburg, Carl. *Abraham Lincoln: The Prairie Years and the War Years, Illustrated Edition.* Edited by Edward C. Goodman. New York: Sterling, 2007.

Sullivan, George. *In the Wake of Battle: The Civil War Images of Mathew Brady.* New York: Prestel, 2004.

Swanson, James L. *Manhunt: The 12-Day Chase for Lincoln's Killer.* New York: Harper Perennial, 2007.

Wills, Garry. *Lincoln at Gettysburg: The Words That Remade America.* New York: Touchstone, 1992.

Lincoln Quotations and Their Sources

The quotations that appear within the boxes on each spread are all Abraham Lincoln's own words. I have provided the exact source for these quotations whenever possible. However, some of Lincoln's most famous words have been passed down from remembered conversations and undated or informal notes. I have provided as complete information as I could find for each quotation.

Page 4: The Gettysburg Address, November 19, 1863

Page 6: First Political Announcement, *The Sangamo Journal*, March 9, 1832

Page 8: Letter to Albert G. Hodges, April 4, 1864

Page 10: Letter to Jesse W. Fell, December 20, 1859

Page 12: Conversation with Dennis Hanks, 1823

Page 14: Conversation with John P. Gulliver, March 10, 1860, as published in *The Independent*, September 1, 1864

Page 16: Letter to Henry L. Pierce and others, April 6, 1859

Page 18: Letter to Isham Reavis, November 5, 1855

Page 20: Notes for a Law Lecture, July 1, 1850 (unconfirmed date)

Page 22: Letter to Mary S. Owens, May 7, 1837

Page 24: Casual conversation at a White House reception, exact date unknown

Page 26: Letter to John Stuart, January 23, 1841

Page 28: Address in Independence Hall, February 22, 1861

Page 30: Conversation with William Herndon in 1858, exact date unknown

Page 32: Letter to Anson G. Henry, after his failed race for Illinois Senator in 1858

Page 34: Exact source unknown, but widely attributed to Lincoln

Page 36: Farewell Address at Springfield, Illinois, February 11, 1861

Page 38: Cooper Union Address, February 27, 1860

Page 40: Remarks at Painesville, Ohio, February 16, 1861

Page 42: Remark made to a delegation visiting the White House, 1863

Page 44: Letter to Grace Bedell, October 19, 1860

Page 46: Speech to the One Hundred Sixty-sixth Ohio Regiment, August 22, 1864

Page 48: Letter to Fanny McCullough, December 23, 1862

Page 50: Comment made en route to Gettysburg, November 18, 1863

Page 52: Letter to George B. McClellan, October 13, 1862

Page 54: Conversation with Illinois congressman Isaac Arnold, May 1864

Page 56: Conversation recalled by Frederick Seward, son of Secretary of State William Seward, at the signing of the Emancipation Proclamation, January 1, 1863

Page 58: Letter to George G. Meade, July 14, 1863

Page 60: The Gettysburg Address, November 19, 1863

Page 62: Proclamation of Thanksgiving, October 3, 1863

Page 64: Conversation with Daniel Sickles, July 5, 1863

Page 66: Reply to Delegation from the National Union League, June 9, 1864

Page 68: Speech in Bloomington, Illinois, on May 29, 1856

Page 70: Letter to William T. Sherman, December 26, 1864

Page 72: Farewell Address at Springfield, Illinois, February 11, 1861

Page 74: Conversations with Mary Todd Lincoln and Ward Hill Lamon, first week of April, 1865

Index

This book is dedicated to the memory of Jack Naylor

Text copyright © 2008 by Martin W. Sandler

All rights reserved. No part of this book may be reproduced or transmitted in any form or by any means, electronic or mechanical, including photocopying, recording, or by any information storage and retrieval system, without permission in writing from the publisher.

First published in the United States of America in 2008 by Walker Publishing Company, Inc.
Visit Walker & Company's Web site at www.walkeryoungreaders.com

For information about permission to reproduce selections from this book, write to Permissions, Walker & Company, 175 Fifth Avenue, New York, New York 10010

Library of Congress Cataloging-in-Publication Data
Sandler, Martin W.
Lincoln through the lens : how photography revealed and shaped an extraordinary life / Martin W. Sandler.
p.   cm.
ISBN-13: 978-0-8027-9666-0 • ISBN-10: 0-8027-9666-4 (hardcover)
ISBN-13: 978-0-8027-9667-7 • ISBN-10: 0-8027-9667-2 (reinforced)
1. Lincoln, Abraham, 1809–1865—Pictorial works. 2. Lincoln, Abraham, 1809–1865—Portraits. 3. Presidents—United States—Pictorial works.
4. Presidents—United States—Portraits. 5. Photography—United States—History—19th century. I. Title.
E457.6.S26 2008   973.7092—dc22   [B]   2008000219

Book design by Alyssa Morris
Typeset in Monotype Fournier and P22 Dearest Script
Printed in China
2 4 6 8 10 9 7 5 3 1 (hardcover)
2 4 6 8 10 9 7 5 3 1 (reinforced)

All papers used by Walker & Company are natural, recyclable products made from wood grown in well-managed forests.
The manufacturing processes conform to the environmental regulations of the country of origin.

Acknowledgments

As always, many thanks are due Carol Sandler, particularly for her informed suggestions, her typing and retyping of the manuscript, and her continuous support. I am also grateful for the valuable help I received from Katherine Worten; Mary Kate Castellani; and my agent, John Thornton. I am most appreciative of the beautiful design that Donna Mark and Alyssa Morris brought to this book, as well as the assistance I received from Mark Lewis of the Library of Congress, James Cornelius of the Abraham Lincoln Presidential Library and Museum, and Linda Suit of the Illinois Heritage Preservation Agency. And I owe many thanks to historian *par excellence* Russell Potter for so thoroughly checking the accuracy of this book. Finally, I owe an enormous debt of gratitude to Emily Easton, whose guidance in shaping this volume, aid in picture selection, and editing skills have made this book possible.

Picture Credits

Courtesy of Abraham Lincoln Presidential Library & Museum (ALPLM): pages 20, 21, 35, 36–37, 85; *detail by The Center for Civil War Photography:* page 61 (inset); *courtesy of Illinois Historic Preservation Agency:* pages 19, 83; *courtesy of Library of Congress:* front cover, front and back endpaper photo, title page, pages 3, 6, 7, 8, 9, 10, 12, 13, 14, 16, 17, 18, 22, 23, 24, 25, 26 (top), 27 (top), 29, 30, 31, 32, 33, 34, 38, 39, 40, 41, 42, 43, 44, 45 (both), 46, 47 (both), 48, 49, 50, 51, 52, 53, 54, 55, 56, 57, 58, 59, 61, 62, 63, 64, 65, 66, 67, 68 (all), 70, 71, 72, 73, 74, 75, 76, 77 (both), 78, 79 (all), 81, 82, 84, 86, 87, 88, 89, 90, 94, 96, back cover and back flap; *courtesy of National Archives:* front and back endpaper text, pages 4, 5 (top), 11; *courtesy of the Naylor Collection:* page 28; *reproduced by permission of the Norman Rockwell Family Agency, Inc:* page 15; *Credit: Picture History:* page 69; *courtesy of Solomon D. Butcher Collection, Nebraska State Historical Society:* page 91; *courtesy of Wikimedia Commons:* pages 26 (bottom), 27 (bottom), 80, 92

As I would not be a _slave_, so I would not be a _master_. This expresses my idea of democracy— Whatever differs from this, to the extent of the difference, is no democracy—

A. Lincoln—